ALSO BY JOHN ELDER

Learn Ruby On Rails For Web Development

PHP Programming For Affiliate Marketers

The Smart Startup: How To Crush It
Without Falling Into The Venture Capital Trap

Adsense Niche Sites Unleashed

Social Media Marketing Unleashed

SEO Optimization: A How To SEO Guide
To Dominating The Search Engines

Intro To Ruby Programming Beginners Guide Series

John Elder

Codemy.com

Las Vegas

Intro To Ruby Programming
Beginners Guide Series

By: John Elder

Published By Codemy.com
Las Vegas, NV USA

ISBN
978-0-692-71441-6

First Edition

http://www.Codemy.com

FOR LULU

TABLE OF CONTENTS

ABOUT THE AUTHOR 15

INTRODUCTION.. 16

    Do you need To Learn Ruby to Use Rails 16

    Get the Book Videos For Free 18

    Grab the PDF version of this book 19

    Conventions Used in the Book 20

    Exercises 20

CHAPTER ONE 22

    Setting Up A Ruby Development Environment 23

    Windows / Mac/ Linux 23

    Mac 23

    Linux 24

    Windows 25

    Cloud Based Dev Environment 26

    C9.io 27

    Getting Started with C9 28

    C9 Text Editor 32

    C9 Directory Tree 32

    C9 Terminal 34

CHAPTER TWO 37

    Writing Our First Ruby Program 38

    Hello World! 39

    Creating a Ruby File 40

    Puts vs Print 42

    Errors 44

    Comments 46

    Exercises 50

CHAPTER THREE **51**

    Fun With Math, Variables, and Inputs 52

    Basic Math Operators 52

    Math With Quotes? 54

    Integers and Floats 56

    Inline Math 58

    Comparison Operators 59

    Variables 62

    Math with Variables 64

    String to Integer 65

    Adding Strings 65

    Multiplying Strings 66

    Assignment Operators 67

    Getting User Input 70

    Getting Numbers As User Input 71

    Exercises 73

CHAPTER FOUR **74**

    If/Then/Else Statements 75

    Basic IF/THEN Statements 76

    IF/ELSE 77

    IF/ESLIF 78

    Multiple Conditionals (| |, &&) 79

    String Manipulation 81

    downcase, upcase, capitalize, reverse, chomp, length 82

    Build A Choose Your Own Adventure Game 84

    Exercises 87

CHAPTER FIVE **88**

    Arrays 89

    Creating an Array 89

    Arrays Start With Zero! 90

    Putting Numbers and Variables Into Arrays 90

    Another Way To Create an Array 91

Adding Stuff to Arrays Later On 92

Removing Items From an Array 94

Multi-Demensional Arrays 95

Exercises 98

CHAPTER SIX **99**

Loops 100

What Is A Loop? 100

While Loops 101

Infinite Loop Problems! 103

Until Loop 106

For Loops 107

Each Loop 109

Fizz/Buzz Game 112

Exercises 117

CHAPTER SEVEN **118**

Methods (Functions) 119

Creating a Method 119

Calling a Method 120

Passing Things Into A Method 120

Fizz/Buzz Using Methods 121

Returning True or False 122

Passing More Than One Argument To A Method 124

Using Default Arguments In A Method 124

Exercises 126

CHAPTER EIGHT **127**

Hashes 128

Hashes vs. Arrays 128

Pizza Hash 129

Hash Keys and Values 129

Calling a Value From Our Hash 130

Adding And Removing Items From a Hash 130

Odds and Ends 132

Alternate Ways To Write A Hash 133

Hash.new 134

When to Use A Hash vs. An Array 135

Exercises 137

CHAPTER NINE **138**

Putting It All Together To Make a Flashcards Game 139

Quick Recap 139

Mapping out our Game 140

Creating Random Numbers 141

start_game method 143

Math Methods 144

add_flashcards Method 145

subtract_flashcards Method 148

multiply_flashcards Method 149

divide_flashcards Method 150

Simplifying The Code 151

Exercises 153

CHAPTER TEN **154**

Conclusion 155

Get My Ruby Video Course Free at Codemy.com 155

A Special Favor 156

APPENDIX A **158**

Get a Massive Discount For My Online Code School 158

INTRO TO
RUBY PROGRAMMING

BEGINNERS GUIDE SERIES

ABOUT THE AUTHOR

John Elder is a Web Developer, Entrepreneur, and Author living in Las Vegas, NV. He created one of the earliest online advertising networks in the late nineties and sold it to publicly traded WebQuest International Inc at the height of the first dot-com boom.

He went on to develop one of the Internet's first Search Engine Optimization tools, the Submission-Spider that was used by over three million individuals, small businesses, and governments in over forty-two countries.

These days John does freelance web development work, writes about Programming, Growth Hacking, and Internet Advertising, and runs **Codemy.com** the online learning platform that teaches Coding, Growth Hacking, and Internet Marketing, and to thousands of students.

John graduated with honors from Washington University in St. Louis with a degree in Economics. He can be reached at john@codemy.com

INTRODUCTION

"Do I need to learn Ruby in order to use Rails?"

Over at Codemy.com I've taught thousands of people how to develop web apps using Ruby on Rails and if I've heard that question once, I've heard it a hundred times.

It's confusing – there's no doubt about it!

Rails is the framework, but *Ruby* is the programming language that Rails was built on. So which is more important to learn? Strangely enough, you don't really need to know Ruby in order to use Rails.

To build a website with Rails, you're mostly working with HTML, CSS, maybe some Javascript...and that's about it.

That's the great thing about Rails – you don't need to know much programming in order to build really *really* cool things very quickly.

So that brings us back to the question: do you need to learn the Ruby programming language in order to build really cool stuff with Rails.

Answer: No!

But *SHOULD* you learn Ruby?

Answer: Absolutely!

If you've got a great idea for some hot new web app and just want to bang out a quick proof of concept website that you can show investors in order to raise VC money, then no; you probably shouldn't waste your time learning Ruby.

But if you're serious about this stuff...if you want to consider a career as a web developer, or want to get a high-paying job as a Rails Developer, or if you're just curious about technology – then you should absolutely take the time to learn Ruby.

It'll make you a better Rails developer, it'll make you a better overall developer; and let's face it – Ruby is just a lot of fun!

So that's what this book is going to do – teach you the basics of the Ruby programming language.

We won't talk much about Rails throughout this book. Heck, we might not talk about it at all.

We won't be building a web app in this book. If you want to learn Rails and build cool stuff check out my book on Rails called "Learn Ruby On Rails For Web Development" over at Amazon. It's been the number one best-selling Rails book off and on over at Amazon since I published it.

In that book I teach you Rails by building a clone of the website Pinterest and you follow along and build your own copy. It's a lot of fun.

In this book we're just going to learn Ruby.

If you already know a programming language, then this will be easy for you because Ruby is much like any other modern programming language.

If you've never programmed anything before, then this will be easy for you. Why? Because Ruby is a pretty easy programming language – that's part of what makes it so fun to use. I'll take things slow.

If you get confused or stuck along the way you can always head over to Codemy.com and use the contact form to get shoot me a message. You bought this book, so I'm happy to help explain anything in here that you don't understand.

FREE STUFF

Everyone learns differently. Some people learn by reading, some by watching and listening, others learn by doing. I want you to be able to learn this stuff in the best way *for you*.

So I've created a companion video course that goes along with this book. Basically it covers everything that the book covers, it's just in video format.

Normally I charge $45 for the course on its own, but I want you to have it for free today as my thank you for giving this book a try.

You can sign up and access the course at Codemy.com/ruby

It's totally free, just use coupon code **rubywow**. I recommend you go sign up right now, because even if you don't watch the videos, by signing up you'll get a membership account at Codemy.com and you can post questions directly to me under each video.

So if you don't understand something in the book, maybe the video will clear things up for you. If not, you can post a question right there and I'll answer personally.

It's not a bad deal for free ;-)

FREE PDF VERSION OF THE BOOK

Programming books are tricky. I like reading my programming books in the paperback form. But you can't copy and paste code from a paperback.

Then there's Kindle...which is super convenient and sometimes does allow you to copy and paste (sometimes – programming books are sometimes different). But the problem with Kindle is that the formatting sometimes messes things up and makes it hard to read...especially code examples etc.

PDF is the best of both worlds. You can read it on your Kindle or iPad or whatever, you can read it online, you can print it out if you want. You can copy and paste code examples, etc. etc. etc.

So everyone who signs up for the free Ruby course at **Codemy.com/ruby** will also get a free copy of this book in pdf form.

Like I said, I want to give you all the tools you need to learn this stuff, so giving you a free pdf copy makes sense to me.

Grab it now at:

http://Codemy.com/ruby

And use coupon code **rubywow** at checkout to get the $0 price.

CONVENTIONS USED IN THIS BOOK

This is a book on Ruby programming, so there will be lots of code examples and snippets.

Usually when I'm just talking about something, things will look like this; regular text in paragraph form.

Whenever there's code to be discussed, I'll use a `fixed width font like this` with a bold header like this:

```
CODE EXAMPLE 2.1
1.
2.    if weather == "sunny"
3.      puts "Go for a run!"
4.    elsif weather == "rainy"
5.      puts "Go to the gym!"
6.    else
7.      puts "Watch TV."
8.    end
9.
```

It should be pretty obvious :-p

I'll also use images from time to time. Hopefully the images will be clear and readable, but if not then get the pdf copy over at Codemy.com/ruby or watch the videos.

EXERCISES

At the end of each chapter or major section of the book, I'll try to give you some practice exercises covering whatever we just discussed. By no means do you need to do all the exercises, but I do recommend that you give them a try.

Even if you think you totally understand the thing I just discussed, there's something about trying it yourself. Don't just go back to what you just read and copy and paste my example code and then modify it to fit the answer.

Instead, I suggest you do the exercises from scratch. Write out all the code by hand, don't copy and paste anything. And maybe wait a little while after you read before trying the exercises.

Ruby is pretty easy. The exercises will likely seem pretty easy, especially after you've just read about them. Instead, wait a few hours, or a day or two and then try the exercises. Give yourself time to forget what you just learned so that you have to reinforce things in your mind by learning it again.

I think you'll get more out of this book that way, and isn't that the whole point? Sure you can speed through this book in a couple of hours, but it won't stick with you the same way.

Ok, enough with this jibber jabber...lets dive in and learn some freaking Ruby!

CHAPTER ONE

SETTING UP A RUBY
DEVELOPMENT ENVIRONMENT

First things first! Before we do any Ruby coding, we need to set up a development environment so that you can actually execute Ruby code.

It's a small but important step!

Windows / Mac / Linux

Running Ruby is different depending on which operating system you're running. As with most things code related, Mac is going to be a little easier out of the box than Windows.

But in this case, it's not a big deal.

Remember, we're focusing on Ruby the programming language, not Ruby on Rails the framework. That means that we don't need to install Rails (which is a nasty, horrible, mind-destroying process that I avoid at all costs). Instead, we just need the Ruby programming language installed on your computer (and not even that if we use a cloud development environment which I'll explain later).

MAC

Good news! If you're running a Mac then you already have Ruby installed on your computer. Don't believe me? Open up a Terminal and type:

```
CODE EXAMPLE 1.1
1.
2.  Ruby -v
3.
```

Punch in that command and hit enter and the terminal should respond with a version number. That means that Ruby is ready to go. It may not be the latest version of Ruby (they're always updating and releasing new versions), but it will probably work just fine for our purposes here.

If you want to download and install the latest greatest version of Ruby, well do that on your own time. We've got more important things to worry about!

Google it or check out the Ruby website:
https://www.ruby-lang.org/en/documentation/installation/

Apart from Ruby, you'll most likely also need some sort of text editor so that you can actually write Ruby code. Any text editor will do. I like Sublime Text 2 and a lot of coders use it. It's free. Google it.

But as I alluded to earlier, we're going to be using a free cloud Ruby development environment in this book. So don't stress over any of this nonsense just yet.

LINUX

Like Macs, Ruby is likely already installed on Linux already. You can open a terminal and check for sure:

```
CODE EXAMPLE 1.2
1.
2.   Ruby -v
3.
```

If the terminal spits out a version number, then you're good to go. If your particular flavor of Linux doesn't have Ruby installed already then you'll need to download and install it.

I'm not going to explain how to do that – let's face it, you're running Linux so you're a badass already who doesn't need my help installing some trifling software!

But in case you can't figure it out, check out the Ruby website: **https://www.ruby-lang.org/en/documentation/installation/**

You'll also need a text editor, I like Sublime Text 2 but use whatever you like. You're running Linux, so I know you'll do exactly that!

But like I mentioned earlier, we're going to be using a free cloud dev environment throughout this book – so you don't really need to do any of this stuff.

WINDOWS

Windows is never particularly friendly to the coder. They always do things their own way – which usually pisses me off because I like to do things MY own way and this can lead to friction.

But in this case, running Ruby on Windows isn't particularly troublesome. In fact, it's downright easy.

Head over to the Ruby Installer website at: **http://rubyinstaller.org**

There you can download the free self-contained Ruby installer for windows. It's one file, download it and double click it to install Ruby.

Like I've mentioned for Mac and Linux, you'll also need some sort of text editor to write code in. Any text editor will work (even Notepad), but I suggest Sublime Text 2 – which is free and many many many coders use it.

But as I mentioned earlier, we're going to use a free cloud development environment to code for the rest of this book.

So you don't need to install Ruby on your computer, or install a text editor.

In fact, let's dispense with these shenanigans and just move right over to this cloud dev environment that I keep yapping about.

CLOUD DEVELOPMENT ENVIRONMENT

Cloud dev environments are relatively new. We didn't really have them even a couple of years ago.

These days, they're the only thing I use.

Why? Because all my code is right there in the cloud instead of stuck on a particular computer. So I can code at home, I can code from the office, I can code at Starbucks, I can code on the plane (as long as there's Internet access of some sort).

In short, you can code from anywhere, at any time using a cloud dev. environment.

What's more – other people can collaborate with you. You can work on code from your house while your buddy helps out from half way around the world.

Not to mention the fact that you don't have to worry about downloading and installing things. I just spent the last 3-4 pages explaining how to install Ruby on different types of operating systems. It's a waste of time.

With a cloud dev environment, it doesn't matter what type of computer you're on. Just fire up a web browser and log into your dev environment and start coding. It's great!

WHICH CLOUD DEV ENVIRONMENT TO USE

There are a lot of cloud development environments to choose from these days. Most of them are free. Well – free for personal use. If you have a team of coders all working on something and you want them to collaborate, you usually have to pay for that sort of thing.

But personal use is almost always free on most providers.

In this book we'll be using Cloud Nine. You can check them out at:
C9.io

I've been using this dev environment for a couple of years now and I really like it. They do everything right, and it's totally free.

Head over to c9.io and sign up for an account. They'll send you a confirmation email with a link to confirm your account. Click the link and log into the site.

John Elder

GETTING STARTED WITH CLOUD NINE

Now that you have your free C9.io account, go ahead and log in and you'll see a screen that looks a little something like this:

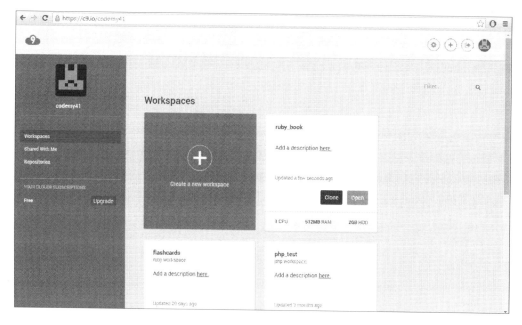

Image 1-1

...or something like that. They're always changing the layout, and you can see that I already have a few projects in my account. Did I mention you can have multiple projects in your account?

The important thing to look for is the "Create A New Workspace" button. It's the big dark grey thing with the + plus sign in the image above.

Go ahead and click that button and create a new Workspace. Once you do, this page will pop up:

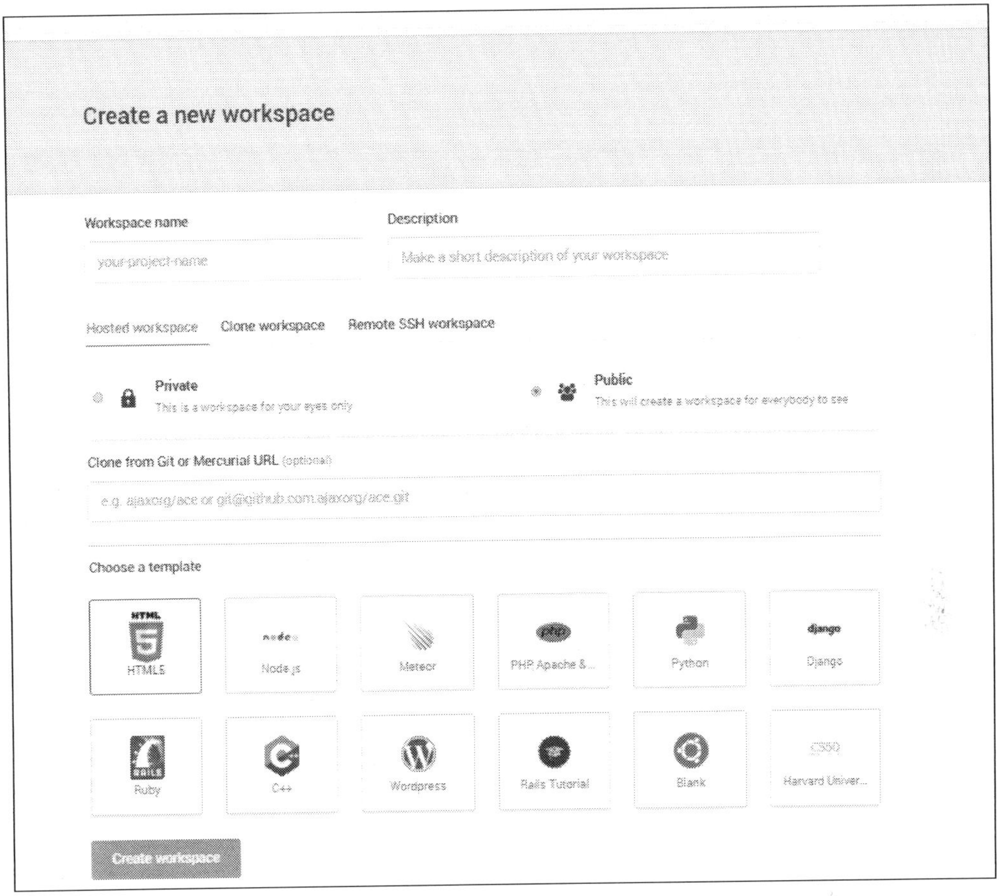

Image 1-2

It's pretty straight forward, first name your workspace. You can call it anything you want; I called mine ruby_book. You can leave the Description field blank.

Next you'll notice the option for private or public, and that public is chosen by default. That means people can see your workspace, though I'm not really sure how they would find it. I believe you have to pay to keep your workspace private, and for learning purposes we don't really care if someone stumbles upon our workspace and sees it. So leave it as Public.

If you're cloning a github repository (we'll talk about version control and github a little later) you can enter the URL of your repository there. We can ignore that because we aren't cloning a repository.

Finally, and this is the most important part, you need to select which type of workspace to create by choosing a template. You can see they have templates for many major programming languages and frameworks; including HTML5, Node, Meteor, PHP, Python, Django, Ruby on Rails, C++, Wordpress, Rails Tutorial, Blank, and Harvard CS50.

There are probably two templates that catch you eye; Ruby on Rails and Rails Tutorial.

Don't fall into that trap!

We're using Ruby – the programming language; NOT Ruby on Rails the framework.

So we don't want to select EITHER of those options (not the Ruby on Rails or the Rails Tutorial template).

Frankly, we could choose them – but then you're going to get a full on Rails development environment and that would be MASSIVE overkill for us at this point and it would probably just confuse you.

Instead, we're going to choose the "BLANK" template.

So go ahead and click the Blank template icon, then click the "Create Workspace" button.

Wham zoom, that's all there is to it! It takes a few moments for C9.io to create your workspace. They're basically spinning up a linux instance that you'll use. It can take a few seconds – up to a minute or so depending on how busy the site is. Once your workspace is ready, it'll look a little something like this:

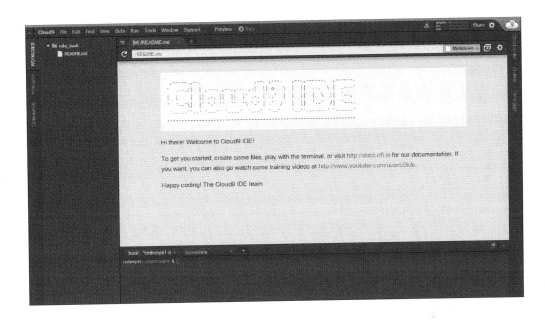

Image 1-3

So let's take a moment to check out this thing! There are basically three main areas that we need to focus on: the file directory on the left hand side of the screen, the text editor right in the middle, and the terminal down along the bottom.

TEXT EDITOR

First things first, let's look at the editor. You can see there's a big obnoxious Readme file open by default. See the tab right above it that says [M]README.md with a little x next to it (sort of like a browser tab)? Any time you open a file, another tab like that will pop up, so you can open multiple files at a time and click through them by clicking the tab at the top of the screen there.

Let's get rid of that Readme.md file by clicking the little x on the tab. As soon as you click the x, the file disappears.

FILE DIRECTORY TREE

Now let's check out the file directory on the left hand side of the screen.

You'll see that there's a main directory, in my case it's called /ruby_book because that's what I named my project. Underneath that you can see that there's exactly one file, README.md.

If you double click that file name, the README.md file pops back up in the editor in the middle of the screen.

This directory acts like a normal windows directory might act. You can add files to it by hovering your mouse there and right clicking, and selecting "new file". You can add a new folder the same way. You can also delete files by right clicking them and choosing "Delete".

In fact, let's do that right now by deleting that stupid README.md file. Click on the file name to select it, then right click and choose "Delete". You'll get a little error warning asking you if you're really really sure you want to delete the file. Confirm and delete. Piece of cake.

TERMINAL (COMMAND LINE)

Finally, let's take a look at the terminal down at the bottom of the screen:

Image 1-5

This is a full on Linux terminal, just like you would see on a Linux machine or on a Mac. One of the reasons why a cloud development environment is so powerful is because you get access to the terminal. You can use any command line command you would use in Linux right here.

If you aren't familiar with the command line or a terminal, don't worry. We won't be using the terminal for much more than running our Ruby files. You'll also see the output of the file right there.

You can change the size of the terminal screen by grabbing the side of it with your mouse and dragging to resize. You might want to do that later when we start running our Ruby files and you want to see the output more easily.

Important

Before we go any further, we need to navigate around the terminal a bit so that we're in the right directory to run our soon to be created Ruby files.

Click on the terminal and enter this command:

```
CODE EXAMPLE 1.3
1.
2.  pwd
3.
```

Then hit enter. Hopefully it should output something that says /home/ubuntu/workspace

If so, everything is fine. That "workspace" directory is actually our ruby_book directory. You actually need to be in the right directory in order to run files in that directory (well, usually at least).

SUMMING UP

So basically that's the C9.io cloud development environment. It might not look like much yet, but once we start making Ruby files and executing code, you'll see how cool it is.

The neat thing about this is that you can just close your browser when walk away whenever you want. The next time you log in, your workspace will look exactly as you left it. All your code will be right there, accessible from any computer with an Internet connection and a web browser.

So spend a minute more looking around. Familiarize yourself with things. Granted, there's not much to see there right now, but in the next chapter we're going to dive in and write our first Ruby program.

Let's get to it!

CHAPTER TWO

WRITING OUR FIRST RUBY PROGRAM

Alright! Let's get write some Ruby code! When you use a framework like Rails, you'll often write Ruby code right there on the web page of whatever site you're building.

But we're not using Rails – and we're not building a web site or web app or whatever you want to call it. We're just going to be writing some basic Ruby code in order to learn the language.

So we need to create an actual Ruby file. Ruby files generally end in .rb so let's create one right now called hello.rb

To do this, fire up your C9.io workspace and hover the mouse over the left hand side of the screen by the directorty tree. Right click and select "New File" from the little menu that pops up.

A new file will appear in the directory, rename it hello.rb and click enter. The screen should look something like this:

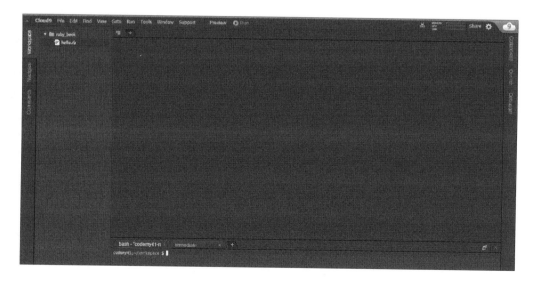

Image 2-1

See the little image of a ruby next to the hello.rb file? That means that C9.io realizes that this is going to be a Ruby file. It probably knows that because we named it with a .rb file extension.

So far so good...now double click that little icon and the file itself will open in the text editor.

There's nothing there now, but let's type in our very first line of Ruby code, which will be the first line you write in ANY programming language, the infamous "Hello World!" line...

```
CODE EXAMPLE 2.1
1.
2.   puts "Hello World!"
3.
```

Type that in and then save the file. You can save it two ways; either by clicking the CTRL+S button on your keyboard (Command S on mac – I believe), or by clicking the "File" link at the very top of the screen, and then choosing "Save" from the menu that pops up.

Your screen should look a little something like this now:

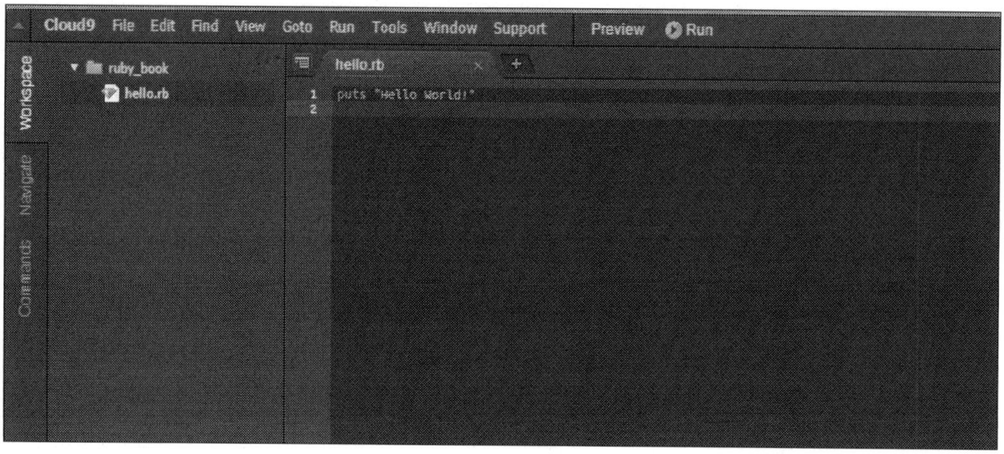

Image 2-2

With me so far? Before we talk about the code, let's run this thing and see what happens! There are basically two ways to run our code. First, since this is the only file we currently have in our project, we can click that "Run" button right there at the top of the screen.

If you do that, another little terminal window will pop up down at the bottom of the screen and it will output some weird messages and then run the file and output it's contents. I don't really recommend you do that, because it's sloppy. Though I guess at this point it doesn't really matter. But later on as we add more files to our directory, that Run button may not know which file to run.

Instead, I recommend that you use the second method. Click down in the terminal and type in this command, then hit enter:

```
CODE EXAMPLE 2.2
$.
$.   ruby hello.rb
$.
```

This should output the line Hello World! right into the terminal.

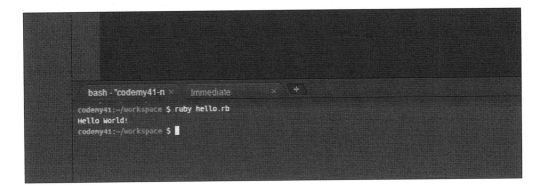

```
bash - "codemy41-n ×    Immediate              ×   +
codemy41:~/workspace $ ruby hello.rb
Hello World!
codemy41:~/workspace $ █
```

Image 2-3

The command "ruby" that we typed tells the terminal to execute the file hello.rb, so whenever you want to run a Ruby program, just type in ruby file_name.rb and the file will get executed and output right there on the screen.

Remember earlier when I told you that you can resize the terminal window? Once our programs get a little more complex, there may be multiple lines of output and you may want to resize that screen so that you can see it all.

THE CODE

So we created our first Ruby program! Congratulations! Sure it was pretty easy, but it was still a pretty impressive thing. Most people don't know how to do even that much in Ruby – and now you do.

So what's going on in our code? Well, not much. We have just one line and the only thing that looks unfamiliar is the word "puts", which I guess tells the Ruby interpreter to "put" something on the screen; in our case we're "putting" the sentence "Hello World!" onto the screen. That sentence is a string (more on strings later).

Notice anything after the last quotation mark in "Hello World!"? Nope, there's nothing else there. In some programming languages you have to end each line with a semi-colon ; or maybe a colon : or something else.

Not so in Ruby, which makes code much easier to read.

CHANGING THINGS UP

Let's play around with our code a bit. There's a couple of different ways to output text to the screen in Ruby. Instead of puts, type in print instead:


```
CODE EXAMPLE 2.3
1.
2.   print "Hello World!"
3.
```


Be sure to save that file, and then run it again in the terminal (type in ruby hello.rb and hit enter like before).

Notice anything different? The first time we ran our code, the line "Hello World!" was outputted on its own line in the terminal. This time, it got squished out all on one line, with the command prompt right after it:

```
bash - "codemy41-n ×    Immediate        ×   +
codemy41:~/workspace $ ruby hello.rb
Hello World!codemy41:~/workspace $
```

Image 2-4

What's going on here? When you use "puts" the thing you want to output gets put on the screen with a line break after it. When you use "print", the thing you want to output gets printed on the screen without a line break.

Why would you use one over another? Lots of reasons. But for now, it's not all that important. We're just playing around with some beginning code.

TERMINAL NOTE

I should mention that you can clear the screen in the terminal by typing in: clear and then hitting enter. You're going to want to do that from time to time because as we continue to run code and output the contents to the terminal screen, things can get a little jumbled up and cluttered feeling.

I usually clear the screen before running any code.

ERRORS

So far, our code has been incredibly simple, so you probably didn't run into any errors. That won't stay the same for very long. If there's one thing that's as certain as death and taxes, it's that you're going to screw something up in your code and get an error.

In fact, let's create an error right now just to see what happens. First, let's change our code back to "puts" (instead of print), but let's also leave off the last quotation mark after "Hello World!"

```
CODE EXAMPLE 2.4
1.
2.   puts "Hello World!
3.
```

Save the file and run it in the terminal.

What happened? Did the code execute? Nope, you got an error code that looked something like this:

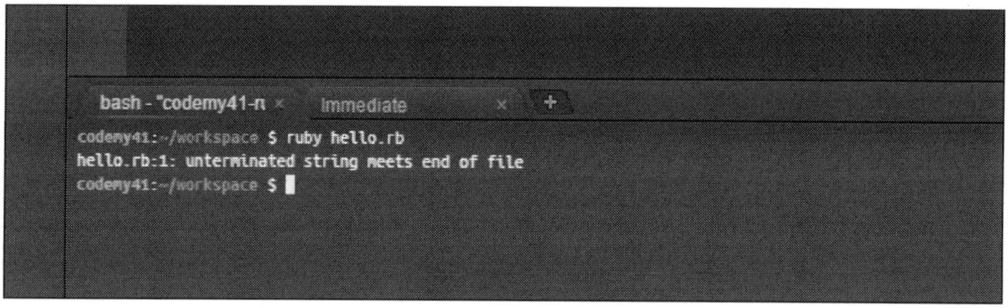

Image 2-5

Hello.rb:1: unterminated string meets end of file. What the heck does that mean? I have no idea! But it seems bad. In our particular case, it just means that we forgot to put the closing quotation mark in there.

But this is the common situation you'll see whenever you screw something up. The code generally won't execute in the terminal and instead you'll get some sort of error.

Get used to it - it's going to happen a lot.

I mean a lot.

So many times.

Welcome to being a coder. Right now, it was incredibly easy for us to figure out what went wrong. A quick glance at our code would have told us that we forgot to type in the closing quotation mark.

But what happens when our code gets more complicated and we have hundreds, or even thousands of lines of code? How do we figure out how to fix it?

Google.

I'm convinced that like 78% of a good developers job is simply Googleing error messages to debug mistakes.

Just copy and paste the error code into Google. I'd leave out the "Hello.rb:1:" part because that only applies to our code (since out file is named hello.rb), instead I'd search at Google for the phrase:
"unterminated string meets end of file"

Sure enough, the results that come up are a suggestion to look for a missing quotation mark.

If you take the time to actually Google this error, you'll see that a lot of the results are from a site called StackOverflow.com

Get used to StackOverflow.com because as a developer, you're going to spend a HUGE amount of time there searching for answers to problems with your code. It's a great resource for coders to ask questions and get help with their code.

Chances are, someone's already had the problem you're having and had their questions answered. So you can read about their solutions right there. If you run up against an error that no one has ever had before, you can post a question, along with your actual code, and people will help you out. All for free.

It's a real community and I highly recommend that you take advantage of it whenever needed.

COMMENTS

Before we move on and start talking about some real coding, I want to mention one more minor thing; comments.

Comments are ubiquitous in any and every programming language. They're everywhere and they're pretty important.

Comments are...well, just that. They allow you to describe your code so that someone else later on can look at it and understand what you've done. They're also for YOU later on when you look back over your code and go "What the heck was that bit of code supposed to do?!"

It's not always obvious what any specific bit of code is supposed to do. That becomes even more true the larger and more complicated your program becomes.

Believe me, if you've been working on a project for three months and have written several thousand lines of code for the thing, you just aren't going to remember what every line is supposed to do.

Sometimes several people hack around on a thing and it gets changed and re-changed a bunch of times. Comments are your friend.

So get into the habit of using comments throughout your code.

You don't have to comment on every single line of code. There are best practices that you'll pick up as you gain experience.

But every time you add a major section to your code, get in the habit of writing a little comment to explain what's going on.

Ruby handles comments with a numbers sign, or pound sign, or whatever you want to call it. # That thing.

Comments get ignored by the Ruby interpreter and don't execute. They're just for our human eyes. You can use them on their own line, or at the end of any line of code.

```
CODE EXAMPLE 2.5
1.
2.  # Output Hello World! to the screen
3.  puts "Hello World!"
4.
```

You see how I put the comment right above the code that I wanted to explain? That's how you do it, but you could also put it at the end of line 3 as well. Like this:

```
CODE EXAMPLE 2.6
1.
2.   puts "Hello World!" # Output Hello World! to the screen
3.
```

Ruby will ignore anything behind the # sign for the rest of the line. Comments can be more than one line too, just use the # sign at the beginning of each line, like so:

```
CODE EXAMPLE 2.7
1.
2.   # This is a comment and it's long
3.   # So I'm going to use two lines for it
4.   puts "Hello World!"
5.
```

Don't get carried away with commenting, you should definitely comment, but keep it short, keep it succinct, keep it direct and easy to read. Don't write a paragraph talking about how you're feeling or what you ate for breakfast.

Here's one more comment use case, take a look at this next bit of code and try to figure out what will happen:

```
CODE EXAMPLE 2.8
1.
2.   puts "Hello World! # I learned about comments!"
3.
```

Can you guess what will be output to the screen? If you guessed:

```
Hello World! # I learned about comments!
```

Then you guessed correctly. Why wasn't that last bit commented out?
Because the # sign was typed INSIDE the quotation marks on line 2.

CHAPTER TWO EXERCISES

1. Write some code that outputs more than one line of text to the screen.

2. Write a comment on the same line as another line of code.

3. Write a multi-line comment

4. Write some code that outputs some text to the screen but doesn't output a line break afterwards

5. Clear the screen of your terminal window in your C9.io development environment

CHAPTER THREE

FUN WITH MATH, VARIABLES, AND INPUTS

Alright, so we've got our cloud development environment all set up over at C9.io and you've familiarized yourself with the whole thing. We've even created our first Ruby program and run it from the command line.

Sure, it was a pretty simple little program, but you've got to start somewhere. So now you know how to create a basic Ruby file and run it, which is pretty important.

It's time to start talking about slightly more complicated things, namely math (and later variables).

Sure, no one really likes math – well I like math – but most normal people don't like math. But math is one of those building block things that you need to master quickly to code in just about any programming language.

Luckily we're not talking about advanced calculus or linear algebra here; we're just talking about basic arithmetic operators like adding, subtracting, multiplying, and dividing.

In this chapter I'll give a quick overview of Ruby's basic math operators.

BASIC MATH OPERATORS

Like I said, we're not going to get into any heavy math right now. We're just going to focus on the basics like addition, subtraction, multiplication, and division.

Math with Ruby couldn't be easier. You might not think you'll use this stuff much because...well...math. But you really will, as we'll see as we go throughout the rest of the book.

Ruby Handles math just like you would expect, with these operators:

- Addition   +

- Subtraction   −

- Multiplication   *

- Division   /

- Modulus   %

- Exponents   **

Those all probably look really familiar to you, except maybe the modulus operator (think remainder), but we'll talk about it in a bit.

For now, let's create a new file called math.rb over at our C9.io workspace. Once you create the file, double click it there in the directory tree to open it. It should be empty.

Let's play around with our math operators.

```
CODE EXAMPLE 3.1
1.
2.  puts 3 + 2
3.
```

Go ahead and save the file, then run it and you should see the number 5 output to the terminal screen. Wow, right?!

There's a couple of things to note here. The first is that we didn't use quotation marks around the 3 + 2. In the last chapter, whenever we used "puts", we slapped a couple of quotation marks around the thing we wanted to output.

Not so with math. But just for fun, try adding the quotes:

```
CODE EXAMPLE 3.2
1.
2.   puts "3 + 2"
3.
```

Save the file and run it. What happened? Instead of outputting 5, the program outputted the text "3 + 5". So if you want to do math, leave the quotes off. If you want to output text, use quotes.

The other thing to not is the spacing. Notice how we used a space between the 3 and the + and the 2?

Those spaces are just for us and our stupid human eyes so that it's easier to read. You could have left them out like this:

```
CODE EXAMPLE 3.3
1.
2.   puts 3+2
3.
```

...and that would get you the exact same output of 5. It's really just a personal preference whether or not you use spaces. Personally, I find it easier to read and therefore easier to keep track of what's going on in my code...so I use spaces.

Play around with the other Math operators. In fact, let's make a little program that uses them all:

```
CODE EXAMPLE 3.4
1.
2.   puts 3 + 2
3.   puts 5 - 1
4.   puts 3 * 4
5.   puts 10 / 5
6.   puts 35 % 3
7.   puts 2 ** 4
```

That should output:

5

4

12

2

2

16

Pretty straight forward, except maybe the modulus operator. **Modulus** basically returns the remainder when dividing the number on the left by the number on the right.

In our example, three goes into thirty-five 11 times (3 x 11 = 33). What's left over? 2 (35 – 33 = 2).

What is 35 % 7? The answer is zero. Why? Because 7 goes into 35 exactly 5 times (7 x 5 = 35) with zero left over.

This might seem a little esoteric, but you'll actually use this thing from time to time because it's helpful to determine programmatically whether a number is fully divisible by another number for a bunch of different reasons that we'll get into later.

INTEGERS AND FLOATS

So we've talked about the basic math operators, now let's talk about numbers in general. This is kind of important.

A number can be an integer or a float.

An integer is a whole number. 5 is an integer. So is 55378008. 98 is also an integer. Whole numbers.

A float is a number with decimals in it. Like 5.27, that's a float. 98.1 is also a float. So is 1,902,488,278,211.923

This is important to understand because Ruby handles floats and integers very differently. Let's take an example:

```
CODE EXAMPLE 3.5
1.
2.  puts 10 / 3
3.
```

Go ahead and run that code. What did you get? You got the answer "3"!

3?

Yep, 3. This seems a little strange to me because 10 divided by 3 is certainly not 3! If I pull out my handy calculator (don't you carry a calculator around with you?!) and divide 10 by 3, I get 3.3333333333 as the answer.

So why did Ruby round down and just tell me the answer was 3? This is a computer, after all, and computers are supposed to be smarter than that!

The answer is integers and floats.

Ruby gave us the integer answer (the number without decimals) and Ruby will always round down when given the chance to do some rounding.

Why did Ruby give us an integer answer? Because we asked it an integer question! Our code was puts 10 / 3 and both 10 and 3 are integers, so Ruby replied with an Integer answer. To get an accurate answer, we need to use floats in our code, like this:

```
CODE EXAMPLE 3.6
1.
2.  puts 10.0 / 3.0
3.
```

If we save that and run it, Ruby returns 3.3333333335 which is a much more accurate answer.

Sometimes you need precision, sometimes rounding is just fine. Just be sure to remember that Ruby will round down for integers and to use floats when you need exact answers.

GETTING A LITTLE CRAZY

So we've talked about some basic math stuff, and we've talked about strings (remember our first program had a string that said "Hello World!" in it).

So let's put the two together and see what we can do. Let's create a math program that outputs all the math operators we've seen so far, with strings as well:

```
CODE EXAMPLE 3.7
1.
2.   puts "3 + 2 = #{3 + 2}"
3.   puts "5 - 1 = #{5 - 1}"
4.   puts "3 * 4 = #{3 * 4}"
5.   puts "10 / 5 = #{10 / 5}"
6.   puts "35 % 3 = #{35 % 3}"
7.   puts "2 ** 4 = #{2 ** 4}"
8.
```

Go ahead and save that and then run it and you should see this output:

- 3 + 2 = 5
- 5 - 1 = 4
- 3 * 4 = 12
- 10 / 5 = 2
- 35 % 3 = 2
- 2 ** 4 = 16

So what's going on here? Well we wrapped everything after our puts in quotation marks. Normally when we use quotation marks like that, no math will get executed. But we wrapped out math in what looks like a comment (which is also pretty weird because # are supposed to be for comments!).

#{....}

Whenever you put that inside a string, Ruby escapes it out of the string and executes the code inside the curly brackets.

Why did we do this? Just for fun! Plus I think it's more readable when you run the program to be able to get the questions as well as the answers. A bunch of numbers outputted to the screen doesn't help me at all. 5...what does 5 mean? But if the program outputs "3 + 2 = 5" then it makes sense to me.

So that's fun. Hey, we're getting a little more complicated here! It's exciting! Well, maybe a little exciting. Let's move on to some slightly more complicated things.

...but we're still going to stick with the math theme for a bit longer because there's a few more math operators that you need to learn, and they're actually really important. You'll use them a lot.

COMPARISON OPERATORS

Comparison operators are something you'll use forever no matter what programming language you code in. Apart from If/Then statements and loops, they're possibly the most used things in all programming.

What are they?

Well, comparison operators are exactly what they sound like...they compare things; two or more things I guess.

Is 5 bigger than 2?

Is 10 equal to 27?

All these things and more can be determined by comparison operators. So here's a list of the biggies:

Table Of Comparison Operators

Equal to	==
Not Equal To	!=
Greater Than	>
Greater Than or Equal To	>=
Less Than	<
Less Than or Equal To	<=

When you use a comparison operator, Ruby will return either "true" or "false", which might seem a little weird at first but totally makes sense.

Give it a try and see:

```
CODE EXAMPLE 3.8
1.
2.   puts 5 > 1
3.
```

If you run that code, the output is "true". Why? Because 5 is greater than 1. Or to put it another way, it is **true** that 5 is greater than 1. Let's make another big batch of code to test out all these operators:

```
CODE EXAMPLE 3.9
1.
2.   puts "5 == 1: #{5 == 1}"
3.   puts "5 != 1: #{5 != 1}"
4.   puts "5 > 1: #{5 > 1}"
5.   puts "5 >= 1: #{5 >= 1}"
6.   puts "5 < 1: #{5 < 1}"
7.   puts "5 <= 1: #{5 <= 1}"
8.
```

Save and run that code and you should see an output that looks like this:

5 = 1: false (because 5 is not equal to 1)

5 != 1: true (because it's true, 5 is not equal to 1)

5 > 1: true (because it's true, 5 is greater than 1)

5 >= 1: true (because it's true, 5 is greater than or equal to 1)

5 < 1: false (because it's false that 5 is greater than 1)

5 <= 1: false (because it's false that 5 is greater than or equal to 1)

Play around with these. Enter different numbers. Enter the same numbers (5 = 5 or 5 != 5) see what happens.

This might not seem terribly important right now, but you really will use this stuff a lot in the future. A lot of coding revolves around comparing different things.

We'll use this stuff soon when we create if/then statements and also loops.

VARIABLES

So far we've just been outputting strings manually to the screen, like "Hello World!" and doing some math and outputting that to the screen. Now it's time to talk about variables.

Variables are like buckets. You can put stuff in them and dump stuff out of them.

In Ruby, you create a variable just by naming it and sticking something in it. Like this:

```
CODE EXAMPLE 3.10
1.
2.   my_name = "John Elder"
3.
```

In that bit of code we created a local variable called "my_name" and we put my name in it. We used an operator to do that, an assignment operator. We "assigned" the string "John Elder" to our variable. We'll talk more about assignment operators in just a minute.

Notice how I named the variable my_name with an underscore. Variable names should be descriptive without going crazy. You wouldn't name a variable this_variable_is_my_name – though I guess technically you probably could.

Keep them short but descriptive, and try to use underscores to separate words in the variable name. You could just as easily have named the variable myname, or MyName though in Ruby we tend to use underscores.

Also keep your variable names lowercase.

Variables are great because from now on within our program, we can use that variable however we want. Let's add another line of code to our program to output my name to the screen:

```
CODE EXAMPLE 3.11
1.
2.   my_name = "John Elder"
3.   puts name
4.
```

Run that program and what do you see? You should see my name.

We don't have to put text in a variable, we can put numbers in them too:

```
CODE EXAMPLE 3.12
1.
2.   my_name = "John Elder"
3.   my_age = 38
4.
```

Notice how I didn't put quotation marks around the number 38? There's a reason. Without quotes, Ruby know that this is a number. That's important because if we wanted to do math with that variable later, we can!

If you put quotes around the 38, then Ruby thinks that you're not using a number, but instead using a string. So if you try to do math with that variable later, you can run into trouble.

In fact, let's try that right now. Create a new program.

MATH WITH VARIABLES

```
CODE EXAMPLE 3.13
1.
2.   number_1 = 5
3.   number_2 = 10
4.   puts number_1 + number_2
5.
```

Run that sucker and see what you get. You should see 15 output to the screen. There's a couple of things to see here. First, you'll notice that we can do math with variables just like we did math with numbers earlier.

Instead of typing 10 + 5 into your program, we assigned 10 and 5 to variables and then did the math on the variables. That's a much better way to do math for a bunch of different reasons.

The second thing to see is that we didn't use quotation marks around either of those two numbers. Just for fun, wrap one of the numbers in quotation marks and then run the program and see what happens:

```
CODE EXAMPLE 3.14
1.
2.   number_1 = 5
3.   number_2 = "10"
4.   puts number_1 + number_2
5.
```

What happened? The terminal threw up a big nasty ERROR and wouldn't add your stuff! The error says "String can't be coerced into Fixnum (TypeError)".

What's going on? Well, our number_2 variable isn't holding a number, it's holding a string. And Ruby won't let you add a number and a string. That would be like telling it to add 27 + apples. What would the answer be? Who knows! You can't add numbers and words.

If you forget, there are ways to convert a string to an integer, that's a little beyond the scope of this intro book, but look up string to integer if you want to see how (actually, we'll discuss it a little later in the book).

APPLES TO APPLES

We've discovered that you can't add numbers and words, but can you add two words with Ruby? Let's see!

```
CODE EXAMPLE 3.15
1.
2.   fruit_1 = "apples"
3.   fruit_2 = "oranges"
4.   puts fruit_1 + fruit_2
5.
```

Care to make a wager what will happen? Will it throw up an error? Actually, it should output this:

applesoranges

As it turns out, a plus sign (+) for strings is used to concatenate the two variables. Whenever we're working with strings and you want to add something in, or concatenate it in, use the plus sign.

```
CODE EXAMPLE 3.16
1.
2.  fruit_1 = "apples"
3.  fruit_2 = "oranges"
4.  puts "I Like " + fruit_1 + " and I like " + fruit_2
5.
```

This bit of code will output "I Like apples and I like oranges" to the screen. Remember earlier when we used #{..}? We can also use variables inside those curl brackets like this:

```
CODE EXAMPLE 3.17
1.
2.  fruit_1 = "apples"
3.  fruit_2 = "oranges"
4.  puts "I Like #{fruit_1} and I like #{fruit_2}"
5.
```

In fact, that way seems a little cleaner to me so I would probably use that instead of a bunch of plus signs. But there are certainly times when either way would be acceptable.

MORE FUN WITH MATH AND STRINGS

Oh we're not done yet! What happens when you try to do other types of math on variables? Let's see!

```
CODE EXAMPLE 3.18
1.
2.  fruit_1 = "apples"
3.  puts fruit_1 * 5
4.
```

Care to wager what will happen? You might be surprised to discover that Ruby will print out apples 5 times to the screen, like this:

applesapplesapplesapplesapples

I really don't know why you'd ever want to do that...but hey, go crazy!

What else works? Well division doesn't work, you'll get an error if you try to puts fruit_1 / 5. You'll also get an error if you try to subtract from apples.

Oddly enough if you use a modulus to puts fruit_1 % 5, Ruby will return apples. I really don't know why!

ASSIGNMENT OPERATORS

We've got one last thing to talk about in this chapter and I left it till last because it has to deal with both numbers and variables and operators.

Assignment Operators are used to assign things. We've seen one already when we assigned a value to our variable using an equal sign (=).

The other main Assignment Operators deal with numbers.

=	Assigns something from the right to the left
+=	Adds and Assigns
-=	Subtracts and Assigns
*=	Multiplies and Assigns
/=	Divides and Assigns
%=	Modulus and Assigns
**=	Exponents and Assigns

So what's going on here. The first one is easy, we already understand that one. But what's going on with these other operators?

I like to call these my lazy operators. Coders are among the laziest group of no-good layabouts on this planet. We want to work as little as possible. That's why we're writing code to do stuff for us. These operators allow me to write even less code. Here's how.

Let's say I have a variable (number_1) and I want to add 27 to it. I could do it like this:

```
CODE EXAMPLE 3.19
1.
2.   number_1 = 14
3.   number_1 = number_1 + 27
4.   puts number_1
5.
```

That's perfectly acceptable. But...well...I had to type out number_1 twice there on line 3. I mean two whole times...I'm too lazy for that! Instead I could have used out += assignment operator like this:

```
CODE EXAMPLE 3.20
1.
2.   number_1 = 14
3.   number_1 += 27
4.   puts number_1
5.
```

If we really want to get crazy, we could leave out line 4 and add it to line 3 like this:

```
CODE EXAMPLE 3.21
1.
2.   number_1 = 14
3.   puts number_1 += 27
4.
```

Now that's much better. Our assignment operator took the value of number_1, added 27 to it, and then assigned that value back to number_1 (erasing the original value that was in there).

All the other assignment operators work the same way. -= subtracts and assigns; *= multiplies and assigns; /= divides and assigns; %= does that weird modulus thing and then assigns; and **= calculates an exponent and then assigns.

You don't need to use manually coded numbers either. You can use two or more variables like this:

```
CODE EXAMPLE 3.22
1.
2.   number_1 = 14
3.   number_2 = 27
3.   puts number_1 += number_2
4.
```

That will add number_2 to number_1 and assign the output to number_1. Remember, whenever you use an assignment operator, the original value of your variable gets erased. It's gone forever, well unless you run the program again :-p

So when we started the program, number_1 was equal to 14. During the program that 14 gets erased and number_1 becomes 41 (14 + 27). Just keep that in mind.

GETTING USER INPUT

Ok, so I know I said that the assignment operators would be the last thing we talked about in this chapter but I just flat out lied. I do that sometimes.

Before we finish this chapter we're going to learn something that's actually fun, and really easy.

So far, when we run our programs they just do something and output something to the screen. We haven't really been able to interact with them at all.

Now we're going to learn how to add input into the program after it starts running. We do this by using something called "gets".


```
CODE EXAMPLE 3.23
1.
2.  puts "What Is Your Name?"
3.  name = gets
4.  puts "Hello #{name}"
5.
```

Give that a run and see what happens. You probably already figured it out; it asks for your name, and then after you type in your name, it tells you hello.

Gets takes user input and assigns it to our name variable. Once assigned, we can use that variable in any way we would normally use a variable.

USING GETS WITH NUMBERS

So this is cool! But what if we want to input numbers instead of words? By default, gets thinks you're entering a string (text) when you enter things. You have to tell it that you're looking for a number (integer). I briefly mentioned this earlier when I told you to go look up string to integer.

Here's how we do it:

```
CODE EXAMPLE 3.23
1.
2.    puts "Enter A Number:"
3.    number_1 = gets.to_i
4.    puts "Enter Another Number:"
5.    number_2 = gets.to_i
6.    puts "#{number_1} plus #{number_2} = #{number_1 + number_2}"
7.
```

Notice how we slapped a .to_i onto the end of each gets? That forces the input to be inputted as a string, which allows us to do math on those variables down there in line 6.

Without it, it would simply output the two numbers you entered. So if you entered a 1 and a 5, the program would output 15 just like it outputted applesoranges earlier when we tried to add those two words (it concatenates them).

So I think we're done with this chapter. You learned about math, math operators, comparison operators, assignment operators, variables, and user input!

We're slowly getting into more complicated and interesting things.

CHAPTER THREE EXERCISES

1. Write some code that outputs your name to the screen

2. Write some code that outputs your name to the screen 10 times using math

3. Write some code that asks how many Apples you'd like to purchase and then output the response

4. Write some code that asks for a person's first name on one line, then after they type it in, asks for their last name. Then tells them "Hello first last name"

5. Write some code that asks (one line at a time) what your name is, where you live, what your phone number is, and what your favorite color is; then outputs all that info to the screen one item per line.

CHAPTER FOUR

IF/THEN STATEMENTS

So we've played with some basic math, and tinkered with variables, now it's time to start with the first of our actual real programming topics. Well, I say real...everything's been real so far; but it's all been really easy so far.

I guess that's not going to change, because IF/THEN statements are really easy too...they just feel a little more *programmy* then things we've done so far.

The great thing about IF/THEN statements is that they give us a lot of power to do all kinds of other things.

I've been writing code since I was seven years old...that's a loooong time. I think IF/THEN statements were one of the first things I ever learned to do. I used them to make "choose your own adventure" games on my Commodore 64 computer.

Choose your own adventure games were actually books we had as kids. "You're standing in front of two doors, one leads left, the other right...to open the door on the left, turn to page 27, to choose the door on the right, turn to page 12".

...That sort of thing. They were all the rage in the 80's but we didn't have the Internet back then, or cell phones; so I guess that's why.

IF/THEN statements allow you to make choices and decisions in your code and do different things based on different things.

"Do different things based on different things"...yeah that makes sense I guess.

Enough jibber jabber, let's just start coding.

IF/THEN STATEMENTS

IF/THEN statements in Ruby are really easy.

```
CODE EXAMPLE 4.1
1.
2.   x = 41
3.   if x == 41
4.     puts "X Does in fact equal 41!"
5.   end
6.
```

So let's look through that code. In line 2 we're just creating a variable (x) and setting it equal to 41.

In line 3 we start our IF/THEN statement. They follow this format:

> *if conditional*
> *   do something here*
> *end*

So in line 3 we look to see if x equals 41 (remember to use double $=$ when checking for equality, not a single $=$ which would assign something).

$x = 41$ is a conditional, but you could use any condition you want (comparison operators are great here). If $x > 2$ that's a conditional. If x != 17...you get the idea.

If line 3 is TRUE (ie if x does equal 41, which it does in our case) then execute line 4. If line 3 is not true (false), then skip line 4 and go right to line 5...which ends out if/then statement (you have to explicitly end an if/then statement).

Pretty simple, right! Let's change line 3 to make it false, just to see what happens.

Can you hazard a guess?

```
CODE EXAMPLE 4.2
1.
2.  x = 41
3.  if x == 42
4.    puts "X Does in fact equal 41!"
5.  end
6.
```

All we did was change line 3 to 42 (instead of 41). When you run that program, nothing happens. Why? Because line 3 gets executed, determines that x does not equal 42, and then ends.

So that's nice, but what if you want to make more than one decision? If x = 41 do this, otherwise do something else? Enter the **IF/ELSE** statement!

```
CODE EXAMPLE 4.3
1.
2.  x = 41
3.  if x == 41
4.    puts "X Does in fact equal 41!"
5.  else
6.    puts "X Does NOT equal 41!"
7.  end
8.
```

When we run this code, we get "X Does in fact equal 41!" because x does equal 41 in this example. If we changed line 2 to another number, say 42, and ran the code again, we would get "X Does NOT equal 41!".

John Elder

Play around with it. You'll use IF/ELSE statements a lot...I mean a LOT.

IF/ELSIF

To throw just a little more complexity into the mix (and give you one more tool that's pretty useful) we can use the IF/ELSIF statement. This allows you to test against a second condition.

Sometimes people get a little confused with this one, but it's not too bad, and actually really helpful. Before we talk about it, let's just take a look.

```
CODE EXAMPLE 4.4
1.
2.   name = "John"
3.   if name == "Bob"
4.     puts "Hi there Bob!"
5.   elsif name == "John"
6.     puts "What up John!!"
6.   else
7.     puts "I don't know who you are!"
8.   end
9.
```

So we set our variable to "John" line 3 checks to see if our name is Bob, it's not so it moves down to line 5, where we give it another conditional to check for. That's our elsif. In this case our variable is in fact "John" so this program will print out "What up John!!" and then end.

If we changed the variable to "Ralph", then the program would print out "I don't know who you are!"

We can slap in as many elsif's as we want, so you can check against as many different things as you can dream up.

MULTIPLE CONDITIONALS

So far we've only been testing one conditional in our if statements, but you can test more than one, using things line AND and OR.

```
CODE EXAMPLE 4.5
1.
2.   name = "John"
3.   if name == "John" or name == "Bob"
4.     puts "Hi there John or Bob!"
5.   end
6.
```

Notice the simple difference in line 3? We slapped an "or" in there and added another conditional to test against. In this case, if our variable is either John OR Bob, the program will return "Hi there John or Bob!"

Instead of or, we could have used "and" as well. For and to be true, our variable would have to be both John and Bob...which I don't really think that's possible. So our program would return nothing in that case.

AND OR

You can use the word "and" or the word "or" here, but you can also use symbols (and you probably should, the less code you use the better – and there are other reasons that you don't care about at this point in your education).

&&   for and

| | for or

So using symbols, our code would look like this:

```
CODE EXAMPLE 4.6
1.
2.   name = "John"
3.   if name == "John" || name == "Bob"
4.     puts "Hi there John or Bob!"
5.   end
6.
```

Notice line 3 is the only difference. We swapped in | | in place of "or".

You could basically do the same thing with an If/elsif statement like this:

```
CODE EXAMPLE 4.7
1.
2.   name = "John"
3.   if name == "John"
4.     puts "Hi there John or Bob!"
5.   elsif name == "Bob"
6.     puts "Hi there John or Bob!"
7.   end
8.
```

...but that's a whole lot more code. We always want to write as little code as possible, both because we're all lazy and also because code bloat is a real problem. Keeping things as simple and easy to read is a really important thing. Don't use six lines of code when you can use four.

CHOOSE YOUR OWN ADVENTURE

Alright, let's take what we've just used and build our own simple little choose your own adventure game.

Before we start, I want to share one little trick that's going to be pretty important for our game (and really any time you input user data).

Let me ask you this; if we build a choose your own adventure game that asks someone to pick a direction – left or right – and our user types in LEFT (all capitals) or Left (first word capitalized)...what happens?

We'll be running an if/then statement to check if their input says "left" or "right" but that's not the same as "LEFT" or even "Left". Computers seem smart, but they really aren't. You have to be explicit.

So we need to make sure that the thing a user types in will be matchable by our program. That's easy enough if we standardize our input.

STRING MANIPULTION

Ruby makes this very easy. We'll just take the user input and change it to lowercase. But how? Ruby has lots of methods for manipulating strings. Here's a few fun ones.

Table 4.1 String Manipulation

81

.downcase	Convert to all lowercase
.upcase	Convert to all uppercase
.capitalize	Capitalize just first letter
.reverse	Reverses string
.swapcase	Switches capitalized to lowercase & vice versa
.length	Returns character length
.chomp	Removes trailing spaces

So how do we use these? We can use them a bunch of ways. We can use them when we first input the user data using "gets", or we can use them on the variable name anytime, or we can use it when we output results using puts. Here's how:

```
CODE EXAMPLE 4.8
1.
2.   puts "Enter Your Name:"
3.   name = gets.downcase
4.   puts "Hi #{name}"
5.
```

In this example we changed the input to lowercase right away, the moment the user typed it in. We could also change the variable anytime like this:

```
CODE EXAMPLE 4.9
1.
2.   puts "Enter Your Name:"
3.   name = gets
4.   name = name.downcase
5.   puts "Hi #{name}"
6.
```

In example we changed the variable in line 4. A better way to do that is to use a shorthand for line 4 like this:

```
CODE EXAMPLE 4.10
1.
2.    puts "Enter Your Name:"
3.    name = gets
4.    name.downcase!
5.    puts "Hi #{name}"
6.
```

Finally, another way to do it is by not changing the variable at all, and instead just outputting it lowercased:

```
CODE EXAMPLE 4.10
1.
2.    puts "Enter Your Name:"
3.    name = gets
4.    puts "Hi #{name.downcase}"
5.
```

Any of these ways will work (and there's probably a bunch of other ways too), you just need to use the one that fits your program the best. In the case of our choose your own adventure game, I'd probably just change to lowercase as soon as the user inputted it.

Refer back to table 4.1 and play around with the other string manipulation methods I showed you.

The chomp one might be confusing. When you use gets, a single whitespace gets added to the string.

So if I typed in john using gets, how many characters would there be in my name variable? J-O-H-N is four characters...but there's actually five! Because gets slaps a whitespace (a single blank space) there at the end (or maybe it's a line return or something like that – whatever).

Using chomps removes trailing spaces from your variable. Give it a try using the .length method.

Did you notice the difference between .capitalize and .upcase? .capitalize just capitalizes the very first word while .upcase capitalizes all the letters in all the words of your string.

So with .capitalize john elder becomes John elder and with .upcase it becomes JOHN ELDER.

Here's some fun homework...how do you capitalize the first letter of all the words in a string? It's a little tricky, but I'll let you Google it (because as a coder you need to start getting in the habit of Googleing code solutions!)

CHOOSE YOUR OWN ADVENTURE

Ok let's get back to the fun stuff. Let's choose our own adventure. This thing could easily spiral out of control so let's confine it to one question and have that question ask for one of two answers. Sound good?

The goal of our game is to find the Ruby Princess. Isn't that the goal of most games? Yep.

So let's start by asking the users name, chomping it, and converting it to lowercase. And then let's ask our question (be sure to chomp it, and convert it to lowercase right away).

```
CODE EXAMPLE 4.11
1.
2.    system "clear
3.    puts "Welcome To Choose Your Own Adventure!"
4.    puts "The goal is to find the Ruby Princess..."
5.    puts "Enter Your Name:"
6.    name = gets.chomp.downcase
7.    system "clear"
8.    puts "You're standing in front of two doors..."
9.    puts "Do you want the door on the left or right?"
10.   question = gets.chomp.downcase
11.   if question == "left"
12.     system "clear"
13.     puts "You fell into a pit and died! GAME OVER"
14.   elsif question == "right"
15.     system "clear"
16.     puts "Congratulations #{name.capitalize} you found"
17.     puts "the Ruby Princess!  YOU WIN!"
18.   else
19.     system "clear"
20.     puts "Sorry, I don't recognize your response GAME OVER"
22.   end
22.
```

Ok, so there's a couple new things going on here. First off right in line one we see something new (and also line 7, 12, 15, and 19) system "clear". That just clears the screen to make things easier to read.

The other thing you'll notice is how we sort of stacked things onto the gets statement in line 6 (name = gets.chomp.downcase). Yep, you can do that!

You'll also notice that we saved the name variable in downcase so that we could test it against our lowercase if/then statement, but in line 16 we capitalized it again when we output the name onto the screen.

That capitalize statement only capitalizes our name there, it doesn't change the variable.

Finally, you'll notice that we put an else statement there at the end as a catchall in case someone entered something other than "left" or "right" to answer our question. It's always a good idea to think of all the weird ways a user might use your program and try to code to catch all that weirdness!

You can easily expand this game to add more questions and make it more fun to play. But for the purposes of this book I just want to keep it simple and use it as an example.

CHAPTER FOUR EXERCISES

1. Create a simple math flashcard game that asks a user what two numbers added together equal and tell them whether or not they got the answer correct.

2. Write some code that asks for a person's full name (first and last name) and then output their name with both first and last name capitalized

3. Write some code that asks for a person's name and then tell that person how many characters are in their name (added them up manually yourself to see if the answer is correct!)

CHAPTER FIVE

ARRAYS

So we're moving right along! So far so good, right? Nothing too terribly difficult? Good.

In this chapter I'm going to teach you all about Arrays.

People sometimes have a hard time wrapping their head around Arrays. It's ok, they can be a little tricky to understand...but not really. Actually they're pretty simple and they're something you're going to use forever, no matter what programming language you happen to be using.

So what is an Array?

Basically an Array is just a variable...but instead of holding one thing, Arrays can hold many many things.

For instance, imagine we have a variable called "name" and we set it equal to "John".

We already know how to do that, it's drop dead simple. But what if we wanted it to also hold "Tim", "Mary", "Beatrice", and "Bluto"?

A variable can't really do that, but an Array can! And this is very useful.

We create an Array almost the same way we create a variable:

```
CODE EXAMPLE 5.1
1.
2.    names = ["John", "Tim", "Mary", "Beatrice", "Bluto"]
3.
```

Pretty easy! Just stick whatever information you want to put in your array into the bracket [ ] and be sure to separate each item by a comma.

How do we get the information out of our array? Just like this:

```
CODE EXAMPLE 5.2
1.
2.   names = ["John", "Tim", "Mary", "Beatrice", "Bluto"]
3.   puts names[2]
4.
```

Can you guess what line three will print out onto the screen?

Trick question...it's not "Tim" (since it looks like Tim is the 2nd item in our array). The answer is actually "Mary".

Why? Because Arrays start at zero. So "John" is the 0th item in our Array, Tim is the 1st, Mary is the 2nd, Beatrice is the 3rd, and Bluto is the 4th.

Burn that into your memory! ARRAYS START WITH ZERO!

What happens if replaced line three with just puts names (instead of puts names[2])? Our program would simple print out every name in our Array.

PUTTING DIFFERENT THINGS INTO ARRAYS

In the example above we put strings into our Array. We could also put numbers and variables as well!

```
CODE EXAMPLE 5.3
```

```
1.
2.   variable_1 = "Tim"
3.   names = ["John", variable_1, "Mary", 41, "Bluto"]
4.   puts names[1]
5.
```

What did we do here? We put a variable and a number into our Array. If we ran this code, it would print out "Tim" because "Tim" is what's inside variable_1.

Notice how we didn't put quotation marks around variable_1 or the number 41. That's important. If you put quotation marks around them, they become strings, not a variable or a number.

You can put other things in Arrays also (things like methods and objects), but we haven't talked about methods or objects yet so we'll go over that later.

ANOTHER WAY TO CREATE AN ARRAY

There are other ways to create an array, for instance you could create one explicitly by calling "new":

```
CODE EXAMPLE 5.4
1.
2.   names = Array.new(5)
3.
```

Be sure to capitalize "Array.new(5)". With that code we've created a new Array (and called it names) and told Ruby that we're going to have 5 items in our Array (0, 1, 2, 3, 4).

In this case, our Array doesn't actually have anything in it at the moment, but it has space for 5 things whenever we get around to putting things in there.

In fact, you can see how many items are in any given array like this:

```
CODE EXAMPLE 5.5
1.
2.   names = Array.new(5)
3.   puts names.length
4.
```

Line three should output 5 in this particular case.

ADDING STUFF TO AN ARRAY LATER ON

We know how to put stuff in an Array with our code, but what if we want to add stuff later on...or change stuff, or remove stuff? Easy.

In the last code we created an empty Array, let's fill it now:

```
CODE EXAMPLE 5.6
1.
2.   names = Array.new(4)
3.   names.insert(2, "tacos")
4.
```

Using insert, we've put "tacos" into the third spot in our array (remember, start with zero...so 2 is the 3rd spot). Line 2 creates our array and puts 4 empty containers in our array.

Personally, I've never really used the Array.new thing, I've always created my arrays explicitly like we did at the beginning of this chapter.

So what if you created an Array, put a bunch of stuff in it, and then want to add something else later...say, at the end? Let's bring back our original Array and play around with it:

```
CODE EXAMPLE 5.7
1.
2.   names = ["John", "Tim", "Mary", "Beatrice", "Bluto"]
3.   names.push("Toby")
4.
```

Push just slaps another item to the end of your Array. To add something to the beginning of our Array, use "unshit":

```
CODE EXAMPLE 5.8
1.
2.   names = ["John", "Tim", "Mary", "Beatrice", "Bluto"]
3.   names.unshift("Trixie")
4.
```

And if we want to add something anywhere else in our array, we can use insert like we did in code example 5.6 Insert won't write over anything that's already there, it will just add whatever you want to add and then shift everything else down one spot:

```
CODE EXAMPLE 5.9
1.
2.   names = ["John", "Tim", "Mary", "Beatrice", "Bluto"]
3.   names.insert(2, "Trixie")
4.
```

So our Array now becomes John, Tim Trixie, Mary, Beatrice, Bluto.

REMOVING ITEMS FROM AN ARRAY

There's several ways to remove an item from an Array. Imaging we want to remove the last item in our Array:

```
CODE EXAMPLE 5.10
1.
2.   names = ["John", "Tim", "Mary", "Beatrice", "Bluto"]
3.   names.pop
4.
```

This will remove poor Bluto from our Array. It's bad enough they're named Bluto...now we've gone and deleted them!

To remove the first item of an Array, use shift:

```
CODE EXAMPLE 5.11
1.
2.   names = ["John", "Tim", "Mary", "Beatrice", "Bluto"]
3.   names.shift
4.
```

Alas, we removed my name from our Array! Oh the humanity!

If you want to remove an item at a particular spot in our Array (say the second item), use .delete_at:

```
CODE EXAMPLE 5.12
1.
2.   names = ["John", "Tim", "Mary", "Beatrice", "Bluto"]
3.   names.delete_at(1)
4.
```

That will remove poor Tim from our Array (remember, Arrays start at zero – I'll keep reminding you till it's burned in your brain!)

You can also remove a specific item from the Array, for instance a particular name:

```
CODE EXAMPLE 5.13
1.
2.   names = ["John", "Tim", "Mary", "Beatrice", "Bluto"]
3.   names.delete("Mary")
4.
```

That will obviously remove Mary from our Array. BE CAREFUL HERE! If there are more than one Mary's in the Array, delete will remove all of them.

So I'd be cautious using that unless you know there's only one particular item in your Array (or if you don't care that you're deleting all instances of that item in the Array).

MULTI-DIMENSIONAL ARRAYS

Remember when I said that we can put all kinds of things into an Array? Well, it turns out that you can put other Arrays into an Array. Did I just blow your mind?

```
CODE EXAMPLE 5.14
1.
2.   names = ["John", "Mary", "Beatrice", "Bluto", [1,2,3,4]]
3.
```

So let's take a look at that code. You'll see we've got our old normal Array with names John, Mary, Beatrice, and Bluto; but then we've added another thing to the end – another array with the number 1, 2, 3, and 4 in it.

Notice how we separated that second array with a comma, just like we separate everything in our Array with a comma.

So what would happen if we puts our Array to the screen? It would print out our Array as you'd expect:

John
Mary
Beatrice
Bluto
1
2
3
4

So that's cool...but how do we access the stuff in that second Array? It's pretty easy. Let's say we wanted to print out the 3 number in our second array (remember, that's the second item in the second Array because arrays start at zero, even embedded Arrays).

```
CODE EXAMPLE 5.15
1.
2.   names = ["John", "Mary", "Beatrice", "Bluto", [1,2,3,4]]
3.   puts names[4][2]
4.
```

A little weird, but not too bad…right? Our nested Array is the fourth item in our Arrray, and the number 3 is the second item in that Array.

You can nest another Array inside that second Array, and another in that one and another in that one…but you might go a little crazy if you do.

Another way to create a multidimensional Array is by creating a second Array separately and then adding the name of that Array to your original array (in the same way that we added Variables to our Array earlier):

```
CODE EXAMPLE 5.16
1.
2.   numbers = [1,2,3,4]
2.   names = ["John", "Mary", "Beatrice", "Bluto", numbers]
3.   puts names[4][2]
4.
```

See how we created a separate Array called numbers, and instead of manually typing in [1,2,3,4] into our names Array, we just typed in the name of our numbers Array.

If we run this code, we'll get the same "3" answer that we got last time.

CHAPTER FIVE EXERCISES

1. Create an Array with the names of five people you know and output the second name to the screen.

2. Create an Array where the first item in the list is a math problem, like 1 + 1 and the rest of the items are names. Output the first item to the screen. (WOAH, MATH can be an item in an Array?!)

3. Create a multi-dimensional Array with 4 items, and each item is itself an Array containing a person's name, their address, and phone number (make up the info). Output the second Array in your multidimensional Array.

4. Output just the phone number of the third item in your Array from the last question.

CHAPTER SIX

LOOPS

Now we're cooking! We've come a long way, from Math to Variables to IF/ELSE statements, and on through Arrays. You've got the foundations of a pretty solid understanding of basic coding so far, but now it's time to dive into something a little more complicated...Loops.

Ok, they aren't really much more complicated. If you didn't have any trouble wrapping your brain around IF/ELSE statements then you shouldn't have any trouble with simple Loops.

So what is a Loop?

Basically a loop is just what it sounds like...it does something over and over and over and over again...looping through again and again and again, until you tell it to stop.

So like start with the number three. Check to see if three is equals ten. If it doesn't, add one to it, then repeat. Now three has became four, check to see if four equals ten, if not add one and repeat.

Keep looping through that until our number equals ten. Then stop. Or do something else. Or whatever!

That's basically a loop.

You're gonna use loops a lot in programming. They're one of those things you'll just always use. Loops and IF/THEN statements sort of go together. You'll have noticed in my lame loop explanation above that I said the word "If" a bunch of times (if three equals ten, if four equals ten, if, if, if).

Loops need if's to determine whether or not the criteria for the loop has been met yet. So I guess you could think of a loop as a fancy if/then statement that keeps getting called until some criteria is reached.

Every programming language has Loops, in fact they all have a bunch of different loops that you can use, and Ruby is no different. Most programming languages handle Loops in roughly the same manner, so if you know loops in one language, it's easy to learn them in another.

We're just going to cover a few useful loops to get you started, namely **while, until, and for Loops.**

WHILE LOOPS

While loops are pretty simple so they're a good place for us to start. A while loop basically says "While something is true, do something". As soon as the thing stops being true, stop looping. Let's take a look:

```
CODE EXAMPLE 6.1
1.
2.   num = 0
3.   while num < 10 do
4.     puts num += 1
5.   end
6.
```

So what's going on here? A While Loop has this general format:

while conditional [do]
  do something
end

We remember conditionals from back at the beginning of the book, we used them with IF/THEN statements. This is where our comparison operators become handy.

So let's take a look at our code. On line 2 we just create a variable and set it equal to zero. Line 3 is where the loop starts, num < 10 is our conditional.

The loop says "Hey, take a look at num, if num is less than 10, do the code that's in line 4, then check (loop) again".

So the first time we run the program num is zero. Zero is definitely less than ten, so our code executes line 4.

Line 4 takes our variable num and adds one to it. Remember that += operator we talked about a few chapters ago?

You could also write that line of code like this:

puts num = num + 1

but puts num += 1 is more elegant. So when our program first runs, it will check to see that zero is less than ten, then add one to it and print 1 to the screen.

It then loops around and starts over. Now when it checks num, it sees that num equals one, which is still less than ten, so it executes the code and adds one to num, printing out 2 to the screen.

And on and on... so the output of our code looks like this:

1
2
3
4
5

6

7

8

9

10

After the program loops through ten times it stops. Why? Because the tenth time the program looped, num became 10. The next time the program started to loop through it asked itself "Hey, is 10 less than ten?"

10 is not less than 10. 10 is equal to 10, so the program stops.

That's the thing, you see…a while loop just keeps looping until the thing stops being true…*while true* keep on looping!

THE INFINITE LOOP PROBLEM

You want to be careful when you create your loops not to build an infinite loop. It's happened to the best of us (in fact, I accidentally did it earlier when I was writing the code for this chapter!).

So what is an infinite loop?

Well, an infinite loop is a loop that just keeps looping forever. It's conditional never gets met and it just keeps looping and looping and looping and looping for all time.

An infinite loop is not a good thing, they'll more than likely cause your program to crash and can even tie up all the resources on your computer or server – causing it to crash.

Yeah, it happens…and it's pretty easy to do. Here's an example, try to spot the problem here:

```
CODE EXAMPLE 6.2
1.
2.    num = 0
3.    while num < 10 do
4.       puts num
5.    end
6.
```

Did you see it? That's basically the exact same code that we just wrote at the beginning of this chapter, I just left off one little thing.

Line 4...all it's doing is putting out our num variable. It isn't incrementing it by one like it did in the last example.

So what's gonna happen if you run that code? Give it a try! You might as well experience the joy and the terror of an infinite loop...I'll wait while you go run that code.

So what happened? It printed out:

0

0

0

0

0

0

0

0

0

0

0

0

0

Over and over and over again and you couldn't get it to stop, right? Yep.

If you're using your cloud development environment at C9, just close the terminal by clicking the little x at the top corner of the terminal itself. You'll have to open another terminal:

Image 6-1

That will kill your terminal, then you need to open a new one by clicking that little + sign right next to the x you just clicked and choose "New Terminal" from the menu that pops up:

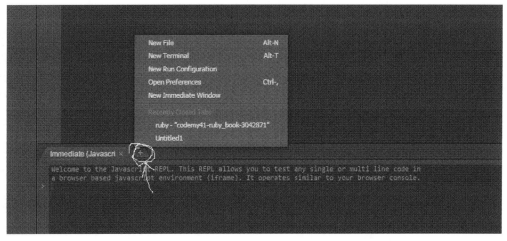

And that fixes that. Fun, right? You're going to create infinite loops, it's just going to happen. You start coding, you get careless...it happens! Just try to keep an eye out for it as much as possible.

UNTIL LOOP

So if a While Loop keeps looping while your conditional is true, an Until Loop does the opposite and keeps looping *until* your conditional is true (or *while* it's false).

The code looks pretty much the same as a while loop:

until conditional [do]
  do something
end

So let's take a look at a basic code example:

```
CODE EXAMPLE 6.3
1.
2.    num = 0
3.    until num == 10 do
4.        puts num += 1
5.    end
6.
```

That will output the following:

1
2
3
4
5
6
7
8
9
10

Just like a While Loop, we have to be careful not to create an infinite loop.

So what's the deal here? While and Until Loops look basically the same right? Well yeah. But as you get into coding there might be circumstances where one of them makes more sense logically to use than the other one. But for the most part it doesn't really matter which you use.

FOR LOOPS

A For Loop is a little different, it runs a specific number of times over a range of numbers; and of course, you specify the range. Check it out:

```
CODE EXAMPLE 6.4
1.
2.  for num in 0..5
3.    puts num
4.  end
5.
```

This will print out:

0
1
2
3
4
5

You'll notice we used num as our variable but we didn't set it to anything. For sets it to iterate over the range that we've speficied (in this case from 0 to 5).

You don't have to use the variable in the output. Often you'll use a For Loop to do something that has to be done many times repetitively. For instance:


```
CODE EXAMPLE 6.5
1.
2.  for num in 0..5
3.    puts "I LOVE CHEESE!"
4.  end
5.
```


...will ouput I love cheese 6 times (from 0 to 5):

I LOVE CHEESE!
I LOVE CHEESE!
I LOVE CHEESE!
I LOVE CHEESE!

I LOVE CHEESE!
I LOVE CHEESE!

I'll be real honest with you...I don't use for loops all that often. You could just as easily use a while or until loop to do the same thing:

```
CODE EXAMPLE 6.6
1.
2.  num = 1
3.  while num < 7
4.    puts "I LOVE CHEESE!"
5.    num +=1
6.  end
7.
```

Granted, that's a whole lot more code than the three lines it took us to do the same thing with a For Loop...and generally less code is better...but whatever.

EACH INSTEAD OF FOR

I think that Ruby coders generally prefer to use Each instead of a For Loop. Each isn't exactly a Loop, it's more of a construct or iterator. But it acts the same way.

> *something.each do |variable|*
>   *code to execrure*
> *end*

So let's take a look at an example:

```
CODE EXAMPLE 6.7
1.
2.   (0..5).each do |num|
3.     puts num
4.   end
5.
```

That's going to output:

0

1

2

3

4

5

You'll notice that it looks an awful lot like a For Loop, just rearranged a bit and simpler. We've designated our range (0 to 5) but we could also use something like an Array to do the same thing:

```
CODE EXAMPLE 6.8
1.
2.   our_array = [0,1,2,3,4,5]
3.   our_array.each do |num|
4.     puts num
5.   end
6.
```

Which would output the same thing:

0

1

2

3

4

5

Being able to easily loop through Arrays and do things is often useful, which is probably why coders like to use Each like this.

You can use the variable (num) to access the items in your Array too:

```
CODE EXAMPLE 6.8
1.
2.   our_array = [0,1,2,3,4,5]
3.   our_array.each do |num|
4.     puts "I LOVE CHEESE #{our_array[num]}"
5.   end
6.
```

Which would print out:

I LOVE CHEESE 0

I LOVE CHEESE 1

I LOVE CHEESE 2

I LOVE CHEESE 3

I LOVE CHEESE 4

I LOVE CHEESE 5

Of course, you could also just do it this way too:

```
CODE EXAMPLE 6.9
1.
2.  our_array = [0,1,2,3,4,5]
3.  our_array.each do |num|
4.    puts "I LOVE CHEESE #{num}"
5.  end
6.
```

I just changed line 4 a bit to only use the variable num instead of our_array[num].

So those are some basic loops. You'll most likely be using Each for the most part, but keep your while and until loops ready because you will use them every now and then!

FIZZ BUZZ

If you've ever gone on a coding interview of any kind, then you've probably had to do some sort of code test to prove your skills. Companies have lots of different puzzles and tests to give you to see whether or not you've got the chops for the job.

Personally I think code interviews are a ridiculous waste of time and an incredibly bad way to choose someone to hire but that's just me.

But I digress...one of the most common code puzzles is the Fizz/Buzz challenge, and now that we know how to do loops and IF/THEN statements, we have all the tools we need to complete this test. So let's take a look!

The problem is simple. Print out every number between 1 and 100, one number per line, but if a number is divisible by three, print out "Fizz" (instead of the number); if a number is divisible by five, print out "Buzz" instead of the number; and if a number is divisible by both three AND five, print out FIZZ BUZZ instead of the number.

Take a minute and think about this problem yourself before reading on. You have all the tools you need in order to do this; and there's lots of different ways to do it.

The idea is to write the most elegant code possible (ie keep it short George!).

How would you do it?

Let's break it down. First things first, we need to loop through the numbers 1 through 100 printing each to the screen. We just learned how to do that no problem.

```
CODE EXAMPLE 6.10
1.
2.   (1..100).each do |x|
3.      puts x
4.   end
5.
```

Now we need to figure out whether any given x is divisible by 3, 5, or both 3 and 5. Sounds like a problem for an IF Statement and a few modulus operators (remember %).

To see if a number is divisible by 3, then the modulus would be zero (no remainders).

```
CODE EXAMPLE 6.11
1.
2.    (1..100).each do |x|
3.      if x % 3 == 0 && x % 5 == 0
4.        puts "FIZZ BUZZ!"
5.      else
6.        puts x
7.      end
8.    end
9.
```

So far so good…line 3 might look a little confusing but it's not too bad. We briefly talked about && earlier (it means AND – it lets you check two different conditions instead of just one).

So line three says basically, if when you divide x by 3 you get a remainder of zero (meaning x is divisible by 3) AND when you divide x by 5 you also get a remainder of zero (meaning x is also divisible by 5) then puts to the screen the words "FIZZ BUZZ!"

Else, just print the number to the screen.

If we run that code, we can spot check that it's working by searching for the first couple of numbers that are divisible by 3 and 5. 15 comes to mind, as well as 30…and I can spot check that our code is printing FIZZ BUZZ! Instead of 15 and 30. So we're good so far.

Now we need to break it down further and check to see if x is divisible by JUST 3 or JUST 5. Sounds like a job for Elsif.

CODE EXAMPLE 6.12

```
1.
2.   (1..100).each do |x|
3.     if x % 3 == 0 && x % 5 == 0
4.       puts "#{x} FIZZ BUZZ!"
5.     elsif x % 3 == 0
6.       puts "#{x} FIZZ"
7.     elsif x % 5 == 0
8.       puts "#{x} BUZZ"
9.     else
10.       puts x
11.     end
12.   end
13.
```

Notice I put a #{x} in there so that it would print out the number as well as the words FIZZ, BUZZ, or FIZZ BUZZ just so we can go through and spot check to make sure the program is doing it's job.

1

2

3 FIZZ

4

5 BUZZ

6 FIZZ

7

8

9 FIZZ

10 BUZZ

11

12 FIZZ

13

14

15 FIZZ BUZZ!

16

17

18 FIZZ
19
20 BUZZ

.

.

.

Yep, looks like it works! And just like that we solved a coding puzzle that has stumped many people in interviews. Don't laugh, I personally know people who have not been able to solve this during an interview.

So we used modulus's and if/then and if/elsif statements, and our basic each loop thing… pretty simple!

I said there are lots of ways to do this…can you think of another way? A simpler way? A way that uses less code? Give it a try…

CHAPTER SIX EXERCISES

1. Do FIZZ/BUZZ again but do it in less lines of code!

2. Create a multi-dimensional Array with 4 items, and each item is itself an Array containing a person's name, their address, and phone number (make up the info). Loop through the Array and output just each person's phone number.

3. Loop through the Array from question 2 and print out the full information of even items in the Array (ie the 2nd and 4th Array in your multidimensional Array).

CHAPTER SEVEN

METHODS (FUNCTIONS)

Now it's time to learn about Methods. Methods are like little programs inside of your program. If you've programmed in another programming language, you probably called these things "Functions", Ruby calls them Functions.

Sometimes I slip and just call them functions...for all intents and purposes they're the same thing.

Methods do specific things, at specific times. In fact, Ruby will ignore any Method you write until you specifically call it. That's different than what we've seen so far.

Up until now, we've written code and whenever we run our program Ruby executes everything we've written and gives us any output that the code creates.

Not so with Methods. You'll see what I mean in a minute. First, let's create our first Method. Methods have the form of:

def name(arguments)
       do stuff
   end

And this basic form should look familiar to you by now...it seems like everything in Ruby tends to look like this. The name should almost always be in lowercase. Let's create an example:

```
CODE EXAMPLE 7.1
1.
2.  def wisdom
3.    puts "You have to know when to hold em"
4.  end
5.
```

Go ahead and run that code and see what happens. Did you run it? Nothing happened! Remember, I told you that Methods don't get executed unless you specifically call them.

To call a Method, just type the name of it. Like this:

```
CODE EXAMPLE 7.2
1.
2.   def wisdom
3.     puts "Life is like a box of chocolates..."
4.   end
5.   wisdom
6.
```

We call the Method on line 5, and if we run this program the output will be: "Life is like a box of chocolates..."

So this is cool, but we've left off part of it...the arguments part. Running a Method that just returns some text isn't very interesting. We want to be able to interact with our Methods, feed them information, have them do something with that information, and then return results based on what it did to that information.

So let's build something more interesting that lets us pass arguments to the Method and have it actually do something.

Hey I know, let's create a Fizz Buzz Method that will tell us if a number is a Fizz or a Buzz (remember in the last chapter fizz numbers are divisible by 3, buzz numbers are divisible by 5, and fizz buzz numbers are divisible by both 3 and five).

We want to be able to pass any number into it and get a result. So let's do that:

```
CODE EXAMPLE 7.3
1.
2.  def fizz_buzz(x)
3.    if x % 3 == 0 && x % 5 == 0
4.      puts "#{x} is FIZZ BUZZ!"
5.    elsif x % 3 == 0
6.      puts "#{x} is FIZZ"
7.    elsif x % 5 == 0
8.      puts "#{x} is BUZZ"
9     else
10.     puts "#{x} is Boring"
11.   end
12.  end
13.
14.  fizz_buzz(97)
15.
```

So basically we're using the same code as in the last chapter when we wrote our Fizz Buzz program, but this time we're building a Method. In line 14 we called the Method and passed the number 97 into it.

Do you see how we pass arguments into the Method? When we define the Method in line 2, we slapped that (x) on there, that's basically a variable. Then when we call the Method in line 14, we designate 97 as the argument we want to pass into the Method. That 97 get's passed into the Method via that (x)...or to put it another way, that x variable becomes 97.

Now anytime within the Method that you see x, our program is putting a 97 in there. Cool!

If you run that code it will return "97 is Boring" because 97 is not divisible by 3, or 5.

If we changed line 14 to fizz_buzz(15) and ran it again, the program would output "15 is FIZZ BUZZ!"

Pretty cool.

Methods are pretty fundamental. They're another one of those things that you're going to use forever, no matter what programming language you end up using (you just might call them 'functions' if you use another programming language). Ruby makes them pretty easy to use, as you've already seen.

So what else can we do with Methods?

RETURNING TRUE OR FALSE

Sometimes it's useful to find out if something is true or false. Lots of times you'll want to do a certain thing if a thing is true, and do something else if a thing is false. So let's create a Method that will return true if a number is even (divisible by two), and return false if a number is odd.

```
CODE EXAMPLE 7.3
1.
2.  def is_even(x)
3.    if x % 2 == 0
4.       return true
5.    else
6.       return false
7.    end
8.  end
9.
10. is_even(99)
11.
```

So what happens when we run that code? Nothing! We get no output. Return doesn't output anything to the screen. Returning true or false may not seem important, but it's something you'll use in the future.

How would you even use this? Lots of ways. You could run an If/Else statement to test for true:

```
CODE EXAMPLE 7.4
1.
2.  def is_even(x)
3.    if x % 2 == 0
4.       return true
5.    else
6.       return false
7.    end
8.  end
9.
10. if is_even(99) == true
11.   puts "TRUE!"
12. else
13.   puts "FALSE!"
14. end
15.
```

Or something like that...you get the idea. Ok, it's a lame example – but trust me, you'll find it useful some day.

Remember our While loop? You can use True or False as the condition in the while loop:

While True
       Do Something
End

So you might use something like this in a While loop.

METHODS CAN HAVE MORE THAN ONE ARGUMENT

Up until now our Methods passed one argument through. But you can pass more than one just as easily:

```
CODE EXAMPLE 7.5
1.
2.  def namer(first, last)
3.    puts "First Name: #{first}"
4.    puts "Last Name: #{last}"
5.  end
6.
7.  namer("John", "Elder")
8.
```

In this program our Method has two arguments (first and last). We call the Method like always, by typing in namer on line 7, but this time instead of passing just one variable, we pass two (in this case John and Elder).

USING DEFAULT ARGUMENTS

The first Method we created back at the beginning of the chapter didn't pass any arguments through. Sometimes you want your Method to use default arguments if none are passed. Let's take a look:

```
CODE EXAMPLE 7.6
```

```
1.
2.  def namer(first = "John", last = "Elder")
3.    puts "First Name: #{first}"
4.    puts "Last Name: #{last}"
5.  end
6.
7.  namer
8.
```

If we run that code it will output:

First Name: John
Last Name: Elder

…notice how we didn't pass any variables when we called the Method in line 7? We just called namer. Since we didn't pass any arguments when we called it, our Method fell back on the default arguments we gave it when we wrote the Method (John and Elder).

Our Method will only use those defaults because we didn't pass any arguments there on line 7. But if we changed line 7 to: namer("Adam", "Smith"), then our program would output:

First Name: Adam
Last Name: Smith

…because we no longer want to use the default John and Elder arguments. Neato.

CHAPTER SEVEN EXERCISES

1. Re-write the fizz_buzz function to prompt a user to enter a number and then return the function result.

2. Write some code using the same fizz_buzz function but have it print out all numbers between 1 and 100 by calling the function 100 times.

3. Create a method that has 7 things passed to it.

CHAPTER EIGHT

HASHES

Now it's time for Hashes…actually, we probably should have talked about Hashes right after we talked about Arrays…because they're very similar.

But I didn't want to confuse you and I wanted to give you enough time to let Arrays sink in.

Remember our names array?

names = ["John", "Tim", "Mary", "Beatrice", "Bluto"]

That's a pretty simple Array, and we access the items in that Array using numbers, starting with zero. So to access the John item in our Array we would do this: names[0] and to access Mary in our Array we would do this: names[2].

To access an item in the Array, we need to know what number it is.

That's fine, there's a lot of times when this will be perfectly acceptable. But when you get right down to it, sometimes being forced to know an item's number position is kind of a hassle.

Enter Hashes.

Hashes are an awful lot like Arrays, but instead of associating an item with it's numbered position; we can associate it with *any damn thing we want!* ™

I don't know about you, but I like having the option to do *any damn thing I want!*™ but then again, I'm 38 years old, live in Las Vegas, and have never had a real job besides running my own startups. So there you go.

By the way; if you want to learn how I build startups and float through life without ever having a real job, check out my site StartupFool.com or grab my "Smart Startup" book or "Living the Dotcom Lifestyle" book from Amazon.

But I digress...Hashes. Let's build one that takes the names from our Array and lists everyone's favorite pizza:

```
CODE EXAMPLE 8.1
1.
2.  favorite_pizza = {
3.     "John" => "Pepperoni",
4.     "Tim" => "Mushroom",
5.     "Mary" => "Cheese",
6.     "Beatrice" => "Ham and Onion",
7.     "Bluto" => "Supreme"
8.     }
9.
10.  puts favorite_pizza["John"]
11.
```

So the first thing to notice is that we wrap our hash in curly brackets { and }.

The next thing to notice is that we separate each value of our hash by a comma.

The items in our hash are called "Keys" and "Values".

With an Array, the "Key" is a number (the 2nd item in the Array, the 4th item in the Array, etc) and that's how we access the items, by calling the number key.

With a Hash, the "Key" is whatever you want it to be. In this case, we're using names as Keys.

So "John" is the Key, and "Pepperoni" is the value. The Value is the thing we want to know.

Calling a value in a Hash is very similar to calling an item in an Array, but instead of referencing an Array number, we reference the Hash Key (like John, or Tim, or whatever).

puts favorite_pizza["John"]

If this was an Array, we'd do something like puts favorite_pizza[0]…but since this is a Hash, we put "John" as the key instead of "0". Make sense?

Hashes are really really cool because you can do most of the things you'd do with an Array, but you can do it in a more human readable and human understandable way. Referencing 0 to see what John's favorite pizza is can be weird, but referencing "John" instead to see what Johns favorite pizza is makes more sense.

ADDING AND REMOVING STUFF FROM A HASH

Just like an Array, we want to be able to remove things and add things to our Hash.

Adding is just as easy as declaring it:

```
CODE EXAMPLE 8.2
1.
2.   favorite_pizza = {
3.     "John" => "Pepperoni",
4.     "Tim" => "Mushroom",
5.     "Mary" => "Cheese",
6.     "Beatrice" => "Ham and Onion",
7.     "Bluto" => "Supreme"
8.     }
9.
10.  favorite_pizza["Bob"] = "Tuna"
11.
```

The important line is line 10. That adds a new key ("Bob") and assigns the value "Tuna" to it. Can you put Tuna on a pizza? Wouldn't that be terrible? Well, Bob's a weird dude.

Deleting things is just as easy, we just use the delete function:

```
CODE EXAMPLE 8.3
1.
2.   favorite_pizza = {
3.     "John" => "Pepperoni",
4.     "Tim" => "Mushroom",
5.     "Mary" => "Cheese",
6.     "Beatrice" => "Ham and Onion",
7.     "Bluto" => "Supreme"
8.     }
9.
10.  favorite_pizza.delete("Tim")
11.  puts favorite_pizza
12.
```

Line 10 delete's the key "Tim" and it's value "Mushroom". We can confirm that by putting out our hash in line 11.

Pretty simple!

HASH ODDS AND ENDS

So far we've been using strings as Keys for our Hash (John, Tim, etc), but you can use other things as well. Things like numbers (though why not just use an Array if you're going to use numbers), and variables:

```
CODE EXAMPLE 8.4
1.
2.   user_name = "John"
3.
4.   favorite_pizza = {
5.      user_name => "Pepperoni",
6.      "Tim" => "Mushroom",
7.      "Mary" => "Cheese",
8.      "Beatrice" => "Ham and Onion",
9.      "Bluto" => "Supreme"
10.     }
11.
12.  puts favorite_pizza
13.
```

In this example the first key is the variable user_name (which we created in line 2 by assigning "John" to the variable user_name). If we run this program we get this output:

{"John"=>"Pepperoni",   "Tim"=>"Mushroom",   "Mary"=>"Cheese", "Beatrice"=>"Ham and Onion", "Bluto"=>"Supreme"}

So even though we used a variable in our code (line 5), the value of the variable becomes the key. Interestingly enough, if you want to access that item of the hash, you can do it two different ways, either by calling it by the variable name (user_name), or the actual value that we assigned to that variable (John).

So you could call it like this:

```
puts favorite_pizza[user_name]
```

or you could also call it like this:

```
puts favorite_pizza["John"]
```

Either way will return the value "Pepperoni". I think that's pretty cool. But then, I've been slamming caffeine pretty hard all morning and I'd think just about anything is cool right now…

ALTERNATIVE WAYS TO WRITE A HASH

Remember when we learned about Arrays and I told you that there's a bunch of different ways to create an Array? Well there's a bunch of different ways to create a Hash.

Before we talk about the different ways to create a Hash, I want to show you a slightly different way to write the Hash we just created. Up until now we've spaced our hash out with a key and value on each line (separated by a comma).

We don't really need to do that, I just like to write them that way because they're easier to read that way. You can write the same exact hash all on one line if you prefer!

```
CODE EXAMPLE 8.5
1.
2.    favorite_pizza = {"John" => "Pepperoni", "Tim" =>
3.    "Mushroom", "Mary" => "Cheese", "Beatrice" => "Ham and
4.    Onion", "Bluto" => "Supreme"}
5.
6.    puts favorite_pizza
7.
```

That does the exact same thing as our earlier code, it's just all jumbled together.

I'm not sure why in the world you'd want to write code that was all jumbled up like that...but hey, go crazy if you feel like it.

I guess if you had a small hash to write with just a couple items, maybe it would make sense to write it all on one line...but even then, why not space things out and make it more readable to us lowly humans?

But this is all just a matter of style; there are actually matters of substance to discuss - because there are actually other *ways* to create hashes.

Personally, I don't think I've ever used another way to create a hash (the way we learned so far is pretty simple, why mess with it?) but I figured I'd mention one or two different ways and you can go Google it if you're interested.

One way is to use the Hash.new class:

```
CODE EXAMPLE 8.6
1.
2.    favorite_pizza = Hash.new
3.
```

That will create a new hash, called favorite_pizza but it'll be empty. Then you have to fill it. So, you know, it doesn't seem that useful.

```
CODE EXAMPLE 8.7
1.
2.  favorite_pizza = Hash.new
3.
4.  favorite_pizza["John"] = "Pepperoni"
5.  favorite_pizza["Tim"] = "Mushroom"
6.  favorite_pizza["Mary"] = "Cheese"
7.  favorite_pizza["Beatrice"] = "Ham and Onion"
8.  favorite_pizza["Bluto"] = "Supreme"
9.
10. puts favorite_pizza
11.
```

Seems a lot sloppier that way, but that's just me. Notice we didn't put commas after each Value ("Pepperoni", "Mushroom", etc). Why? Because we didn't use the old way to create hashes, we used that new way where we create a blank Hash on line 2. The subsequent lines of code are us just adding items to the Hash one at a time. So no commas.

Use whichever method you like to create your own hashes. Like I might have mentioned earlier, I'm all about letting you do *any damn thing you want!* ™ I mean, that's why we're coders!

WHEN TO USE A HASH VS. AN ARRAY

So Hashes or Arrays, which should you use and when? It's pretty straight forward...when you need to access items by a number, use an Array. For all other purposes, use a Hash.

John Elder

To tell you the truth, there's probably times when I've used a Hash even though all my Key values where numbers. You can use numbers in a Hash if you want...so why not? We could just as easily done this:

```
CODE EXAMPLE 8.8
1.
2.   favorite_pizza = {
3.      1 => "Pepperoni",
4.      2 => "Mushroom",
5.      3 => "Cheese",
6.      4 => "Ham and Onion",
7.      5 => "Supreme"
8.      }
9.
10.  puts favorite_pizza
11.
```

I'm not really sure *why* you'd want to do that...but you absolutely could if you wanted to use a Hash instead of an Array.

Just don't try to access the 0'th item of the Hash like you would an Array because there isn't one in this code...unless we specifically named the first item 0!

CHAPTER EIGHT EXERCISES

1. Create your own hash, with five of your friends names and their phone numbers.

2. Create a program using your answer to question 1 where it prompts a user to enter a name (list your five friends) and then returns the phone number for that specific friend.

3. Add a feature to your code from question two that allows people to add or delete a name from the Hash, then return the updated hash to the screen.

4. Do the same thing as question one and two and three but use the alternate stupid method for creating a Hash that we discussed at the end of this chapter.

5. Create a loop that cycles through your hash from question one and outputs (one per line) "My friend X's phone number is: xxx-xxx-xxxx" replacing the x's with the persons actual name and phone number.

CHAPTER NINE

PUTTING IT ALL TOGETHER TO
MAKE A MATH FLASHCARD GAME

Congratulations! You've made it through the book (well mostly) and now you know Ruby!

Well...you know the basics of Ruby...but the basics will take you pretty far. You've got a solid foundation of basic programming concepts and how they're done with Ruby.

We talked about Variables, Math, all kinds of Operators like Math Operators, Comparison Operators, Assignment Operators, and even some Logical Operators (|| and &&).

You learned all about IF/THEN and IF/ELSE statements, Loops, Array, Hashes...we really covered a t lot of good stuff!

I hope you had a good time learning these things and I hope it wasn't too hard...it really wasn't too bad, was it?

Well now it's time to put everything we've learned together and have a little fun.

Right now I'm working on a new course over at Codemy.com that teaches you how to build a children's math flashcard web app that actually speaks the questions to the kids and allows them to speak their answers. It's *really* cool. If you're interested in that I highly recommend you go join my Codemy.com site.

Membership is usually $97 for all the courses (or $45 per course if you take them individually) but sign up using the coupon code **amazonruby** and I'll give you complete access to all the courses (and all the new courses I create) for just $45 total.

But back to us...I thought it might be fun for us to build our own Ruby math flashcard game.

It won't be a web app (like the one I'm building at Codemy.com) and it won't speak the questions and answers...but we can still have some fun banging out the code for just a basic math flashcard game and more importantly, it'll give us a chance to use nearly everything we've learned so far.

A MATH FLASHCARD GAME

Before you build any sort of program or project, it's a good idea to take a few minutes and map out what the program needs to do. I'm just talking broad sketch here.

So what does our program need to do?

Well...we want to build a simple math flashcard game. It should allow the user to choose to do Addition, Subtraction, Multiplication, or Division.

It should then randomly create a math problem and ask the user to solve it. Then it should allow the user to enter their answer and see whether or not the answer was correct or not.

Nothing too tricky here!

Before we get started though, there's one more thing you need to learn...Randomization.

RANDOMIZATION

We're going to need some way to create random numbers for our game. You'd be surprised how often you need to generate random numbers in everyday coding life. Luckily Ruby has an easy way to do it:

```
CODE EXAMPLE 9.1
1.
2.   puts Random.rand()
3.
```

That will generate a random number. Of course, that doesn't really help us because it could be ANY number…like 3990930492423 or .23 and we need to be more specific. So we'll pass a range into our Random method like this:

```
CODE EXAMPLE 9.2
1.
2.   my_rand = Random.rand(0..10)
3.   puts my_rand
4.
```

First off, you'll notice that I slapped a variable on there, so we can do stuff to that number we generate later if we want.

Second off, you'll notice the 0..10 range. So what this range thing does is tell Ruby to return a random number between 0 and 10. It's important to understand this range; Ruby could return 0 and it could also return 10…and any number between.

The two dots between the 0 and 10 are important. Two dots tells Ruby to return a number between 0 and 10 (including 0 and 10). If you put three dots, Ruby will return a number between 0 and ten but NOT including 10. So it would return any number between 0 and 9.

Keep that in mind. I tend to use two dots always. Why? Because if I want my range to not include 10, I'll just change the statement to Random.rand(0..9).

So now we know how to generate Random numbers and slap them into Variables so that we can play around with them.

So let's start building our game!

I highly recommend you try to build this thing on your own without looking at my code. I'm going to suggest how to proceed with each section of the game, and I hope you'll take my suggestions and then write your own code.

Then come back and look at my code to see if I did it the same way. Remember, there's no right way to do this. Your code could look drastically different than mine. That ok! As long as it gets the job done, it doesn't really matter how you do it.

So let's get started…

I think we should break the game apart into different methods that we can call at various times throughout the game. Let's start with a start game method.

Basically, we need to greet the user and ask them what kind of flashcards they'd like to play (Addition, Subtraction, Multiplication, or Division).

This seems like a gets.chomp.downcase sort of thing, and also an IF/ELSIF type of situation. Be sure to put to error handle too (in case the stupid user types in Bacon instead of Subtraction!).

```
CODE EXAMPLE 9.4
1.
2.  # Method To Start The Game And Pick Cards
3.  def start_game()
4.   system "clear"  #clear the screen
5.   puts "Welcome to Math Flashcards!"
6.   puts "Choose your flashcards (add|subtract|multiply|divide)"
7.   pick = gets.chomp.downcase
8.
9.  if pick == "add"
10.   add_flashcards #run addition method
11.  elsif pick == "subtract"
12.   subtract_flashcards #run subtraction method
13.  elsif pick == "multiply"
14.   multiply_flashcards #run multiplication method
15.  elsif pick == "divide"
16.   divide_flashcards #run division method
17.  else
18.   puts "Sorry, I don't recognize #{pick}"
19.   puts "please hit enter to try again"
20.   gets
21.   start_game
20. end
21.end
22.
23. start_game
24.
```

This is how I choose to start things. Can you think of a simpler more elegant way?

So let's look through this code. I started out with a simple comment to describe what's going on here. Don't forget that commenting code is important, especially now that we're building more complicated programs.

I started out defining a method to start the game, called start_game. You'll notice we aren't passing any variables into it. You'll also notice that I've called the method on line 23 (remember Methods don't run until you call them).

Next we've got some code to ask a person what sort of flashcards they'd want, then a simple IF/ELSIF statement to figure out what to do next based on whatever the person typed in.

You'll notice that for each part of the IF statement, I've referenced a method that we haven't written yet. Don't worry, we'll write them next.

The only other thing to really take a look at is the last ELSE statement. That's our error handling. If the stupid user types in NACHOS instead of "add" then our program throws up a statement telling them that we don't recognize their response and asking them to hit enter to start over.

See the naked gets statement on line 20? That just allows the user to hit their enter button on their keyboard. When they do, our program simply executes the next line of code, line 21 which calls the start_game method again (which allows the stupid user to take another swing at picking which flashcards they want to use).

So far so good!

MATH METHODS

Now we need to write the four different math methods; one for addition, subtraction, multiplication, and division.

Basically we need our program to randomly generate two numbers, and then ask the user to either add, subtract, multiply, or divide those two numbers together.

We need to capture their response, and check to see whether they answered correctly or not. If not, we could give them the chance to try again, but in this case I think we'll just tell them that they're wrong and tell them the right answer.

Then we need to give them the option to quit, or get another flashcard. We should probably also give them the chance to switch flashcards completely, ie to switch from Addition flashcards to Subtraction flashcards (or whatever).

So let's start out with the addition flashcards method and then go from there...

```
CODE EXAMPLE 9.5
1.
2. # Start Addition Flashcards Method
3. def add_flashcards()
4.   system "clear"
5.   card_one = Random.rand(0..10)
6.   card_two = Random.rand(0..10)
7.   correct = card_one + card_two
8.   puts "#{card_one} + #{card_two}"
9.   answer = gets.chomp.to_i
10.
11. if answer == correct
12.   puts "Correct! #{card_one} + #{card_two} = #{answer}"
13. else
14. puts "Wrong! #{card_one} + #{card_two} = #{correct}"
15. end
16.
17. puts "Would you like another card? (yes|no|restart)"
18. continue = gets.chomp.downcase
19.
20. if continue == "yes"
21.   add_flashcards
22. elsif continue == "no"
```

```
23.  puts "Thanks for playing!"
24.  exit
25. elsif continue == "restart"
26.   start_game
27. else
28.   puts "Sorry, I don't recognize #{continue}"
29.   puts "please hit enter to try again"
30.   gets
31.   add_flashcards
32. end
33. end
34.
35. # End Addition Flashcards Method
36.
```

First things first; where does this code go? If you put this whole chunk of code BELOW our original start_game method bunch of code, you'll get an error.

Why?

The answer has to do with flow control. If the start_game method is first, it will try to call the add_flashcards method. The problem is; Ruby can't find that method. Why? Because it hasn't gotten down to it yet.

Ruby starts at the top of a program and works its way down. Our add_flashcards method doesn't necessarily have to be above the start_game method, but it DOES have to be above the line of code where we first CALL the start_game method (line 23 in our 9.4 example code).

I tend to put all my methods first before we run any actual code to call a method. That way Ruby runs over all our methods, knows they exist, and feels good about the situation. Then later on when we call one of those methods, everything works the way it's supposed to work.

So let's look at our add_flashcards method.

Most of it should be self-explanatory. Line 5 and 6 gives us our two random numbers and line 7 adds them together so that we know what the correct answer should be. You don't really need to explicitly create a variable with the correct answer, you can do it in the IF Statement, but I like to keep things simple.

Line 9 is where our user types in their answer. Notice the gets.chomp.to_i thing? The .to_i part is important because we're working with numbers here. We need to make sure that ruby realizes that our answer variable is an integer (.to_i stands for to_integer).

After that we just have a series of IF/ELSE statements to check and see whether or not the answer given is correct or not and whether or not the user wants to keep playing or not. Line 24 has an exit statement we haven't seen yet; that just exits out of the statement.

Pretty simple, eh?

Now we can just copy and paste this method to create our other math methods. We'll just need to tweak it a bit so that it subtracts instead of adds; and multiplies or divides or whatever. But I think the basic foundation of the thing is solid.

Wasn't that easy?

Could you have done that just a couple of days ago?

I hope you're starting to understand just how easy Ruby is...and just how much fun it is to use! Sure this is a pretty simple little program, but all programs are simple when you really break them down.

If you understand these basics, you're well on your way to becoming an awesome Ruby coder. Ok enough blather, let's build our subtraction method:

```
CODE EXAMPLE 9.6
1.
2. # Start Subtraction Flashcards Method
3. def subtract_flashcards()
4.   system "clear"
5.   card_one = Random.rand(0..10)
6.   card_two = Random.rand(0..10)
7.   correct = card_one - card_two
8.   puts "#{card_one} - #{card_two}"
9.   answer = gets.chomp.to_i
10.
11.  if answer == correct
12.   puts "Correct! #{card_one} - #{card_two} = #{answer}"
13.  else
14.  puts "Wrong! #{card_one} - #{card_two} = #{correct}"
15.  end
16.
17.  puts "Would you like another card? (yes|no|restart)"
18.  continue = gets.chomp.downcase
19.
20.  if continue == "yes"
21.    subtract_flashcards
22.  elsif continue == "no"
23.    puts "Thanks for playing!"
24.    exit
25.  elsif continue == "restart"
26.    start_game
27.  else
28.    puts "Sorry, I don't recognize #{continue}"
29.    puts "please hit enter to try again"
30.    gets
31.    subtract_flashcards
32.  end
33. end
34.
35. # End Subtraction Flashcards Method
36.
```

All I did was go through the add _flashcards code and replace the plus signs with subtraction signs. Let's do the same thing for the final two math methods and call this sucker done!

CODE EXAMPLE 9.7

```
1.
2. # Start Multiplication Flashcards Method
3. def multiply_flashcards()
4.   system "clear"
5.   card_one = Random.rand(0..10)
6.   card_two = Random.rand(0..10)
7.   correct = card_one * card_two
8.   puts "#{card_one} * #{card_two}"
9.   answer = gets.chomp.to_i
10.
11.  if answer == correct
12.   puts "Correct! #{card_one} * #{card_two} = #{answer}"
13.  else
14.  puts "Wrong! #{card_one} * #{card_two} = #{correct}"
15.  end
16.
17. puts "Would you like another card? (yes|no|restart)"
18. continue = gets.chomp.downcase
19.
20. if continue == "yes"
21.   multiply_flashcards
22. elsif continue == "no"
23.   puts "Thanks for playing!"
24.   exit
25. elsif continue == "restart"
26.   start_game
27. else
28.   puts "Sorry, I don't recognize #{continue}"
29.   puts "please hit enter to try again"
30.   gets
31.   multiply_flashcards
32. end
33. end
34.
35. # End Multiplication Flashcards Method
36.
```

Again, I didn't make any real changes to this code, I just replaced all the signs to multiply. I also changed the name of the method from add_flashcards to multiply_flashcards in a couple places throughout the code. So let's knock out the division code and call it a day!

CODE EXAMPLE 9.7

```
1.
2.  # Start Division Flashcards Method
3.  def divide_flashcards()
4.    system "clear"
5.    card_one = Random.rand(0..10)
6.    card_two = Random.rand(1..10)
7.    correct = card_one / card_two
8.    puts "#{card_one} / #{card_two}"
9.    answer = gets.chomp.to_i
10.
11. if answer == correct
12.   puts "Correct! #{card_one} / #{card_two} = #{answer}"
13. else
14. puts "Wrong! #{card_one} / #{card_two} = #{correct}"
15. end
16.
17. puts "Would you like another card? (yes|no|restart)"
18. continue = gets.chomp.downcase
19.
20. if continue == "yes"
21.   divide_flashcards
22. elsif continue == "no"
23.   puts "Thanks for playing!"
24.   exit
25. elsif continue == "restart"
26.   start_game
27. else
28.   puts "Sorry, I don't recognize #{continue}"
29.   puts "please hit enter to try again"
30.   gets
31.   divide_flashcards
32. end
33. end
34.
35. # End Division Flashcards Method
36.
```

I did need to make a minor change in this code. Check out line 6. I changed the range of numbers for our Random number. Why? Because technically a number can't be divided by zero; and if Ruby tries it will throw a big ugly error. So I just changed the range.

If you run this thing, you'll see a few weird things. You'll see things like 5 divided by 3…and the answer is 1. Since we didn't program in floats or use our modulo (%), our program doesn't know how to deal with remainders.

You'll see things like 0 divided by 7…which is 0.

So, this isn't all that practical. But you can tinker with it and make it smarter if you like…in fact, I'll add that to the exercises at the end of this chapter.

MAKING IT SIMPLER

So we finished the flashcard game! But man, when I add up all the lines of code for this thing, it ends up being like 170 lines! Surely we can simplify things a bit.

One area I would look at for simplification is the math methods. We have four math methods (addition, subtraction, multiplication, division) but each of those methods is essentially the same big block of code (we just change the name of the method and the math operators).

Can you think of a way to reduce those four methods into one method?

There's a bunch of different ways. You could use loops somehow…or make just one method and pass a variable into it as the argument; the variable could be "add", "subtract", "multiply", or "divide" and then based on what that variable is, the method could add, subtract, multiply, or divide.

I'll leave it to you, it's great practice to take some code and try to simplify it!

If you want to get the entire code for this program in an easy to copy and paste format, head over to codemy.com/ruby and sign up for the video course that goes along with this book.

It's usually $45 but as a thank you reading this book, you can get the course for free…just use coupon code **rubywow** at checkout.

Everyone who signs up also gets a pdf copy of this book and you can copy and paste the code right out of there.

I've also listed a pdf of just this program so you can easily see all the code in one place.

Plus, if you have any questions about the code, you can post them there and I'll answer them personally.

CHAPTER NINE EXERCISES

1. Re-Create the flashcards game to keep track of how many questions the user got right and wrong.

2. Re-Create the flashcards game with questions about fractions.

3. Re-Create the flashcards game a different way using less code (make it more elegant Eugene!)

4. Re-Create the flashcards game using While statements to check for correct answers in each of our Math methods (instead of the If statements we're using now).

5. Re-Create the flashcards game, but modify the subtraction method to make sure card_one is greater than card_two (so the answer can't be negative!)

6. Re-Create the flashcards game but clean up the division method so that it makes more sense. Put in logic that keeps picking random numbers until you get one that is divisible by the other one (otherwise it's going to ask you to divide 3 by 9, which is zero or other dumb things like 5 divided by 4, which is 1 and not really correct). Floats? A larger range of Random Numbers? Go crazy!

CHAPTER TEN

CONCLUSION

You made it! We're done! How 'bout them apples?

What'd you think? Ruby's pretty freakin easy – right? Yes it is!

I hope you enjoyed the book, I really enjoyed writing it and head over to Codemy.com/ruby and sign up for my free Ruby course (use coupon code **rubywow**). You can ask me questions directly if you got stuck anywhere along the way.

RUBY ON THE WEB?

Throughout this book we've been playing around with Ruby in the terminal, but we haven't done any web development work with it.

That's because Ruby alone can't easily do web stuff. You need a framework to go along with it…

That's where Rails comes in.

If you're interested in Rails, I hope you'll checkout out my best-selling book "Learn Ruby on Rails for Web Development" at Amazon (http://goo.gl/QpddaH)

(or just go to Amazon and Search for Elder Rails or Elder Ruby or something like that – it'll pop right up).

In that book I walk you step by step to building your first web app with Ruby on Rails. We'll actually build a clone of the website Pinterest. Fully functioning, fully real, fully awesome.

I'll show you how to do everything…and you don't need any special tools or costly web hosting to do it.

I've also got a video course that goes along with the book over at Codemy.com/rails

Close to 4,000 people have taken the course so far and it's gotten overwhelmingly good reviews.

The course normally costs $97 individually, but as another thank you for reading this book I'll give you TOTAL membership at Codemy.com for just $45 (use coupon code **amazonruby** at checkout).

I know it seems like I give out a lot of coupons and stuff, and I do – but it's only because I'm really passionate about this stuff and I want you to have all the tools you need to become a great coder – and I just don't think people should have to spend an arm and a leg on this stuff.

CAN I ASK YOU A <u>HUGE</u> FAVOR?

Book reviews at Amazon.com are a HUGE deal for small writers like me. Just a few reviews can mean the difference between a book getting ranked well by Amazon's algorithm, and complete oblivion. Without reviews the book won't even show up when someone searches for Ruby on Rails at Amazon.

I'd consider it a great favor if you would head back to Amazon.com and leave a quick review of this book. It doesn't have to be long-winded, just a few words will make a big big difference as to whether my book gets out there or not.

So if you enjoyed the book, got a lot out of it...heck even if you didn't like it, please head back to Amazon and leave a review. Then shoot me an email and let me know so I can thank you properly!

Just go to **Codemy.com/rubybook**

And that URL will re-direct to this book's Amazon page where you can leave a quick review.

I really appreciate it!!

Thanks!
-John Elder
Codemy.com
john@Codemy.com

APPENDIX A

SPECIAL CODEMY.COM OFFER

Learning never stops, especially for coders. There's always something new and cool to learn. I've tried to build a website that makes it super easy to learn how to code, and learn new coding skills...and it's called Codemy.com

Each course at Codemy.com is a series of videos where you watch over my shoulder as I build something.

In one course I build a Twitter-like site where people can post anonymous secrets. In other course I build a social network for people looking to start bands. In another course I build an affiliate marketing site that makes money from Amazon affiliate products.

I teach Rails courses, PHP courses, HTML and CSS courses, and more.

Each course costs $97, or you can sign up for all the courses for $197 (which is a pretty good deal if you ask me!) and that entitles you to all the future courses that we add absolutely free (and we've got some cool courses on the horizon).

AS A SPECIAL THANK YOU FOR READING THIS BOOK...

I'd love to see you over at Codemy.com and I'd like to bribe you to join today; so I'm giving you a special coupon code (**amazonruby**) that will give you $152 off membership (so you pay just $45 instead of $197)...

It's my gift to you! **http://www.Codemy.com/**

So you get access to my best-selling course and for just **$45** instead of the regular $197.

And we offer a two month-long 100% money back guarantee. Check out the site, if it isn't for you…just shoot me a message and I'll immediately refund your money, no questions asked, no hoops to jump through.

HANDS ON HELP

Membership doesn't just get you videos…you also get hands on help from me and other members. Any time you get stuck with something, you can post a question to me directly, or post a question in our members forum.

It's a great resource and I hope you'll take advantage of it.

Just use coupon code **amazonruby** at checkout for the special $45 price. **http://www.Codemy.com**

See you on the inside!

-John Elder
Codemy.com

THE END

<u>NOTES</u>

John Elder

NOTES

<u>NOTES</u>

<u>NOTES</u>

NOTES

Made in the USA
San Bernardino, CA
21 August 2018